Contents

Grammar	Communicative Function

Beginning Interactive Grammar

ACTIVITIES AND EXERCISES

Irene S. McKay

George Brown College of Applied Arts and Technology

HEINLE & HEINLE PUBLISHERS
A Division of Wadsworth, Inc.
Boston, Massachusetts   02116   U.S.A.

The publication of *Beginning Interactive Grammar* was directed by the members of the Heinle & Heinle ESL Publishing Team:

David C. Lee, Editorial Director
Susan Mraz, Marketing Manager
Kristin Thalheimer, Production Editor

Also participating in the publication of this program were:

Publisher: Stanley J. Galek
Editorial Production Manager: Elizabeth Holthaus
Assistant Editor: Kenneth Mattsson
Project Manager: Hockett Editorial Service
Manufacturing Coordinator: Mary Beth Lynch
Photo Coordinator: Martha Leibs-Heckly
Interior Designer: Rita Naughton
Illustrator: Susan Detrich
Cover Illustrator: Bonnie Griffith
Cover Designer: Christi Rosso

Photo Credits: Chapter 1 opener—woman studying, Sven Martson, Comstock; woman coaching swimming at poolside, Laimute E. Druskis, Stock, Boston; Laurel and Hardy, Archive Photos. Chapter 2 opener—woman studying, Sven Martson, Comstock; aerobics class, Michael Grecco, Stock, Boston; Laurel and Hardy, Archive Photos. Chapter 3 opener—students going to school, Bryce Flynn, Stock, Boston; Crosby and Hope, Archive Photos; start of a race, Bob Daemmrich, Stock, Boston. Chapter 4 opener—students in a cafeteria, Ulrike Welsch; Charlie Chaplin, Archive Photos; umpire and manager, AP/Wide World.

Heinle & Heinle Publishers is a division of Wadsworth, Inc.

Manufactured in the United States of America

Library of Congress Cataloging-in-Publication Data

McKay, Irene S.
    Beginning interactive grammar : activities and exercises / by
Irene S. McKay.
        p.   cm.
    ISBN 0-8384-3926-8
    1. English language—Grammar—1950– —Problems, exercises, etc.
    2. English language—Textbooks for foreign speakers.   I. Title.
    PE1112.M38   1993
    428.2'4—dc20
                                                                        92-29933
                                                                        CIP

TO MY FATHER AND MOTHER,
STEFAN AND STANISLAWA SADOWSKI,
whose experience as immigrants influenced the course of my life.

CHAPTER 4   Functioning in Conversation   197

Grammar   Communicative Function

Preface

Beginning Interactive Grammar is intended for adults and older teenagers in the beginning stages of language learning. It has been written for both students and teachers to use in a classroom setting. Grammatical explanations as well as communicative activities and more traditional exercises are included. The materials aim to foster a supportive, nonthreatening atmosphere in which learners will feel comfortable enough to engage freely in conversations with one another and with the teacher. The overall goal is to maximize the opportunities for communication by providing the learners with both the means and the motivation for practice.

The second language speaker needs to produce "comprehensible output"—output that is governed by the grammatical rules of the language. However, grammatical competence alone will not enable the second language learner to engage in the wide variety of speech acts required in everyday life. This book contains many practice activities which enable the learner to bridge the gap between knowing the rules and using them in day-to-day communication.

This book provides the teacher with materials to use from the very first day of English classes. In addition to simplified grammatical explanations and examples, open-ended, information exchange activities for pairs, groups, and the whole class are included. Many of these are followed by related writing activities. Some simple reading selections are also provided, along with a number of traditional grammar exercises which allow learners to check their accuracy. This book utilizes the learners' experiences to present and practice grammatical structures. The approach is learner-centered and cooperative, permitting the teacher to act as facilitator and co-communicator in the language learning activities.

The exercises and activities use the idioms and vocabulary of a variety of settings in the urban North American context. This enables learners to acquire an understanding of the culture and to develop an appropriate lexicon.

This book attempts to be as comprehensive as possible, covering almost all the grammatical items and language functions taught to students in the beginning levels of English as a second/foreign language. The materials are intended to provide between 200 and 300 hours of classroom instruction, depending on whether the learners are absolute beginners or only in need of a review of the basics.

Beginning Interactive Grammar includes many different kinds of exercises and activities in order to accommodate diverse learning styles and to promote the development of various language skills. Many activities are intended as whole-class walk-around exercises in which students speak to most of their classmates. These not only produce a warm, cohesive atmosphere in the class, but also generate an enormous amount of language. Other activities have been designated for pair or group work. Even the traditional grammar exercises are intended to be done by pairs so that these too will provide a jumping-off point for discussion in English and further opportunity for practice. Because language is a tool used primarily in communicating with others, the goal of all the activities in this text is *interaction in English*.

To the Student

Beginning Interactive Grammar is a book about English grammar. It is different from other grammar books because it gives you a lot of opportunity to speak to all the people in your class.

These are the goals of *Beginning Interactive Grammar:*

You will practice expressing your own ideas.

You will speak English confidently.

You will understand and engage in basic everyday conversation.

You will understand and use basic everyday vocabulary.

You will understand and use basic English grammar easily.

Beginning Interactive Grammar contains many different kinds of activities. In some you will speak to all the other students in your class. In others you will read or write or practice a grammar point. Most of the time you will do this work with a partner.

There are many good reasons for asking you to work cooperatively with your classmates. First of all, you will get much more practice if you speak to the other students than you will if you speak only to your teacher. In fact, you can get excellent practice by speaking to other learners. This can be just as valuable as talking to native speakers of English because it gives you experience in doing all the things you need to do in day-to-day life, such as expressing your ideas and being able to understand other people's views.

There are further important reasons for working with your classmates. The most significant one is that we can all learn something from one another. If your English is better than your partner's, you will get valuable experience explaining your ideas, making yourself understood, and sharing what you know. If your English isn't as good as your partner's, you will get practice asking questions and confirming information. Last but not least, the more you work with the people in your class, the better you will get to know one another, and the more relaxed you will become about speaking English. Learning English will become fun, and this too will make it easier for you to master the language.

We use language to communicate our ideas and feelings and to share our experiences with one another. Practicing this same kind of communication is probably one of the best ways to learn a language as well. *Beginning Interactive Grammar* asks you to share and to communicate with others as you are learning English. Your participation is the key to success.

Good Luck! I hope you enjoy using *Beginning Interactive Grammar*. I hope you have fun learning English. I know you will be successful.

Acknowledgments

As ESL teachers, we need to have a solid rapport with our learners in order to be effective. Equally, though, we must have a good rapport with our peers and the support of our administrators in order to achieve our goals. I feel that I have been extremely fortunate in having all of these.

I would like to thank the many colleagues and friends with whom I have had the pleasure of working, for making the field of ESL such a rich and stimulating one.

I want to thank George Brown College and Marsha Ann Skolnik, the Chair of the Language Training Department, for the support that I have received.

I owe particular thanks to the many students I have taught in ESL courses and in teacher training programs, for the inspiration they have provided.

I am also deeply indebted to Peter Avery, Martha Low, Terri Massin, and Irene Rich for their helpful comments.

I would also like to thank David Lee and Ken Mattsson at Heinle and Heinle, and Rachel Youngman of Hockett Editorial Service, for their input, advice, and support.

The Basics

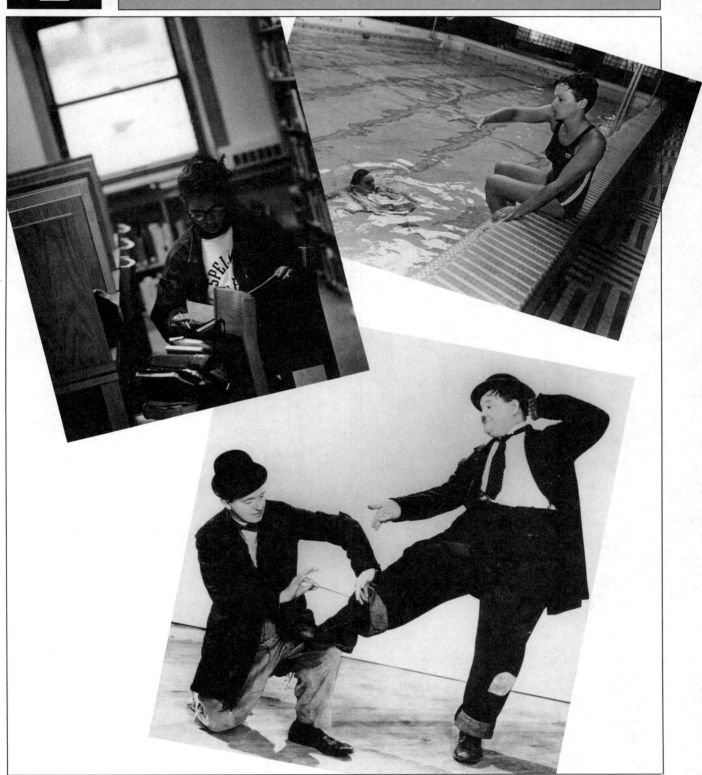

Explanation

When people do not understand words or names, they sometimes ask for the spelling. Each letter of the alphabet has a sound and a name. For example, the sound of the first letter in "teacher" is "t" but its name is "tee." We use this name in spelling words out loud.

Practice A   With your teacher, practice the English alphabet. Circle those letters that are difficult for you.

ENGLISH CONSONANTS		ENGLISH VOWELS	
B	b	A	a
C	c	E	e
D	d	I	i
F	f	O	o
G	g	U	u
H	h		
J	j		
K	k		
L	l		
M	m		
N	n		
P	p		
Q	q		
R	r		
S	s		
T	t		
V	v		
W	w		
X	x		
Y	y		
Z	z		

Practice B With a partner, draw a circle around the words. Spell the words out loud.

```
N  K  S  T  U  D  E  N  T  S  A
O  N  C  T  H  E  I  G  H  P  T
P  T  H  A  T  S  G  X  P  E  N
Q  B  O  O  K  K  H  S  T  L  O
R  W  O  R  D  S  T  O  O  L  T
S  A  L  P  H  A  B  E  T  H  E
```

Practice C Work with a partner.

Spell the name of your school. _____ .

Spell the street your school is on. _____ .

Spell your teacher's last name. _____ .

Spell your teacher's first name. _____ .

Practice D Fill in the information for yourself. Then fill in the information for your partner. Ask these questions:

What is your first name? Please spell it.
What is your last name? Please spell it.
What is your address? Please spell the street name.
What country are you from? Please spell it.

	SELF	PARTNER
First name or given name	_____	_____
Last name or surname	_____	_____
Address	_____	_____
Country	_____	_____

Practice E Stand up. Walk around. Talk to all the people in the class. Ask these questions:

> What is your first name? Please spell it.
> What is your last name? Please spell it.

Write this information in the chart below.

	GIVEN NAME	SURNAME
1.		
2.		
3.		
4.		
5.		
6.		
7.		
8.		
9.		
10.		
11.		
12.		
13.		
14.		
15.		

With a partner, put the first names of all the students in alphabetical order.

1. _____   6. _____   11. _____

2. _____   7. _____   12. _____

3. _____   8. _____   13. _____

4. _____   9. _____   14. _____

5. _____   10. _____   15. _____

Practice F **Outside the Classroom**

Talk to three people not in your class. Fill in the information about them and report to the class.

First name _____

Surname _____

First name _____

Surname _____

First name _____

Surname _____

Practice G   Stand up. Walk around. Talk to all the people in your class. Ask these questions:

> What's your first name? Please spell it.
> What's your address? Please spell the street name.

	NAME	ADDRESS
1.		
2.		
3.		
4.		
5.		
6.		
7.		
8.		
9.		
10.		
11.		
12.		
13.		
14.		
15.		

With a partner, put the street names in alphabetical order.

1. _____   9. _____

2. _____   10. _____

3. _____   11. _____

4. _____   12. _____

5. _____   13. _____

6. _____   14. _____

6. _____   15. _____

8. _____

Lesson 2   CARDINAL NUMBERS

Explanation   We use numbers to give or to get information. These are the numbers in English.

1	2	3	4	5	6	7	8	9	10
one	two	three	four	five	six	seven	eight	nine	ten

11	12	13	14	15	16	17	18
eleven	twelve	thirteen	fourteen	fifteen	sixteen	seventeen	eighteen

19	20	21	22	23
nineteen	twenty	twenty-one	twenty-two	twenty-three

30	40	50	60	70	80	90	100
thirty	forty	fifty	sixty	seventy	eighty	ninety	one hundred

136
one hundred and thirty-six

1990
one thousand nine hundred and ninety

Pronunciation Note

13 thir<u>teen</u>
14 four<u>teen</u>
15 fif<u>teen</u>
16 six<u>teen</u>
17 seven<u>teen</u>
18 eigh<u>teen</u>
19 nine<u>teen</u>

We stress these numbers on the second syllable. We say the second syllable with -<u>teen</u> louder and longer.

30 <u>thir</u>ty
40 <u>for</u>ty
50 <u>fif</u>ty
60 <u>six</u>ty
70 <u>seven</u>ty
80 <u>eigh</u>ty
90 <u>nine</u>ty

We stress these numbers on the first syllable. The first syllable is pronounced louder and longer.

Practice A   With a partner, write out these numbers. Circle the part of the word that is louder and longer. Say the numbers to your partner.

13 _____   16 _____   50 _____   19 _____

30 _____   60 _____   18 _____   80 _____

40 _____   17 _____   70 _____   90 _____

14 _____   15 _____   50 _____   13 _____

Practice B   Write down five difficult numbers or prices. When you finish, dictate them to your partner.

MY NUMBERS   MY PARTNER'S NUMBERS

1. _____   _____

2. _____   _____

3. _____   _____

4. _____   _____

5. _____   _____

When you finish, check your numbers.

How many mistakes did you make? _____

Practice C   With a partner, write out these checks.

1. Consumers' Gas Company
    $230.90

YOUR NAME	583

_____ 19 _____   1-7103 / 2260

PAY TO THE
ORDER OF _____ | $ [   ]

_____ D O L L A R S

RIDGE
SAVINGS BANK ■

FOR _____   _____

⑈ 123045067   876000543 ३⑈ 0583

2. Downtown Fine Cars
   $14,515.30

```
┌─────────────────────────────────────────────────────────────────┐
│         YOUR NAME                                          584    │
│                                                                   │
│                                    _____ 19 ____   1-7103        │
│                                                      2260         │
│  PAY TO THE                                                       │
│  ORDER OF _____ ⌐  $ ┌──────────┐    │
│                                                   └──────────┘    │
│  _____  D O L L A R S │
│                                                                   │
│  RIDGE                                                            │
│  SAVINGS BANK ▪                                                   │
│                                                                   │
│  FOR _____    _____    │
│  ⑈ 123045067      876000543  ⑊ 0583                              │
└─────────────────────────────────────────────────────────────────┘
```

3. Discount Appliance Center
   $3,360.89

```
┌─────────────────────────────────────────────────────────────────┐
│         YOUR NAME                                          585    │
│                                                                   │
│                                    _____ 19 ____   1-7103        │
│                                                      2260         │
│  PAY TO THE                                                       │
│  ORDER OF _____ ⌐  $ ┌──────────┐    │
│                                                   └──────────┘    │
│  _____  D O L L A R S │
│                                                                   │
│  RIDGE                                                            │
│  SAVINGS BANK ▪                                                   │
│                                                                   │
│  FOR _____    _____    │
│  ⑈ 123045067      876000543  ⑊ 0583                              │
└─────────────────────────────────────────────────────────────────┘
```

4. Ed's Bargain Warehouse
   $29.99

```
┌─────────────────────────────────────────────────────────────────┐
│         YOUR NAME                                          586    │
│                                                                   │
│                                    _____ 19 ____   1-7103        │
│                                                      2260         │
│  PAY TO THE                                                       │
│  ORDER OF _____ ⌐  $ ┌──────────┐    │
│                                                   └──────────┘    │
│  _____  D O L L A R S │
│                                                                   │
│  RIDGE                                                            │
│  SAVINGS BANK ▪                                                   │
│                                                                   │
│  FOR _____    _____    │
│  ⑈ 123045067      876000543  ⑊ 0583                              │
└─────────────────────────────────────────────────────────────────┘
```

5. The Campus Bookstore
   $19.59

```
                    YOUR NAME                                    587

                                          _____19_____  1-7103
                                                                 2260
   PAY TO THE
   ORDER OF _____|  $ [            ]

   _____ D O L L A R S

   RIDGE
   SAVINGS BANK ■

   FOR _____      _____

   ⑃ 123045067      876000543 ЗII°  O583
```

6. A.T.&T.
   $319.70

```
                    YOUR NAME                                    588

                                          _____19_____  1-7103
                                                                 2260
   PAY TO THE
   ORDER OF _____|  $ [            ]

   _____ D O L L A R S

   RIDGE
   SAVINGS BANK ■

   FOR _____      _____

   ⑃ 123045067      876000543 ЗII°  O583
```

Practice D   Find out the ages of all the people in your class. Walk around and ask these questions:

> What's your name? Please spell it.
> How old are you?
> What is your year of birth?

The answer to the question "How old are you?" is "I'm 20," or "I'm 20 years old."
Please remember that it is not polite to ask someone's age if you are not good friends.

	NAME	AGE	YEAR OF BIRTH
1.			
2.			
3.			
4.			
5.			
6.			
7.			
8.			
9.			
10.			
11.			
12.			
13.			
14.			
15.			

What is the average age of your classmates? _____

To find the average, add up all the ages of the people in the class, then divide by the number of people.

Example: To get the average of 16, 19, and 22, first add the numbers, 16 + 19 + 22 = 57. Then divide 57 by 3. The average is 19.

Practice E   Stand up. Walk around. Talk to as many classmates as possible. Ask these questions:

> What is your name? Please spell it.
> What is your telephone number?
> What is your address?
> What is your zip code?

	NAME	PHONE NUMBER	ADDRESS	ZIP CODE
1.				
2.				
3.				
4.				
5.				
6.				
7.				
8.				
9.				
10.				
11.				
12.				
13.				
14.				
15.				

Explanation   Pronouns

I   YOU   HE   SHE

THEY   WE   IT

AFFIRMATIVE	CONTRACTIONS	EXAMPLES
I am	I'm	I'm in the classroom.
He is	He's	He's at school.
She is	She's	She's at home.
It is	It's	It's in the library.
We are	We're	We're in the English class.
You are	You're	You're at work.
They are	They're	They're in the cafeteria.

Practice A   With a partner, write a sentence about you.

_____

Write a sentence about your teacher.

_____

Write a sentence about a student in your class.

_____

Practice B   Work with a partner. Use the correct form of the verb *to be*.

1. I ____*'m*____ a student.

2. I _____ in the classroom.

3. He _____ at home.

4. They _____ in the cafeteria.

5. We _____ in the classroom.

6. You _____ at work.

7. It _____ Monday.

8. They _____ teachers.

9. Marie _____ in the cafeteria.

10. She _____ at school.

11. They _____ at work.

12. It _____ at home.

13. He _____ in the library.

14. You _____ students.

15. He _____ a teacher.

16. She _____ in the hall.

17. We _____ at school.

18. John _____ in the library.

Lesson 4	THE VERB *TO BE:* NEGATIVE, LOCATIVES

Explanation

NEGATIVE	CONTRACTIONS	EXAMPLES
I am not	I'm not	I'm not at work.
He is not	He isn't	He isn't at the library.
She is not	She isn't	She isn't at home.
It is not	It isn't	It isn't in the hall.
We are not	We aren't	We aren't in the cafeteria.
You are not	You aren't	You aren't in the office.
They are not	They aren't	They aren't at the bookstore.

Practice A   With a partner, make one affirmative and one negative statement.

1. I ____*'m*____ in the classroom.

   I ___*'m not*___ at home.

2. She _____ in the cafeteria.

   She _____ in the classroom.

3. He _____ at work.

   He _____ at home.

4. They _____ in the hall.

   They _____ in the classroom.

5. You _____ in the building.

   You _____ outside.

6. They _____ in the library.

   They _____ in the bookstore.

7. We _____ at school.

   We _____ at work.

8. George _____ in the corridor.

   George _____ in the men's room.

9. Laura _____ at the nurse's office.

   Laura _____ here.

10. Joe and Susan _____ at home.

    Joe and Susan _____ at the shopping mall.

11. You _____ at school.

    You _____ at work.

12. Susan and I _____ in the computer lab.

    Susan and I _____ in the language lab.

Practice B   Write two negative statements about you.

_____

_____

Write two negative statements about your teacher.

_____

_____

Write two negative statements about two people in your class.

_____

_____

Lesson 5	**THE VERB *TO BE*: INTERROGATIVE**

Explanation   These are the question forms of the verb to be:

QUESTIONS   EXAMPLES

Am I?   Am I in the right place?
Is he?   Is he at school?
Is she?   Is she downstairs?
Is it?   Is it downtown?
Are we?   Are we in the right room?
Are you?   Are you upstairs?
Are they?   Are they outside?

Practice A   With a partner, write out the question forms of these sentences:

1. They're in the cafeteria.   _____Are they in the cafeteria?_____

2. She's in the library.   _____Is she in the library?_____

3. You're at home.   _____

4. She's at work.   _____

5. They're in the ladies' room.   _____

6. Joe's downstairs.   _____

7. Linda and John are in the office.   _____

8. He's at the bookstore.   _____

9. She's downtown.   _____

10. Henry's outside   _____

11. Mary's upstairs.   _____

12. Jason and Jim are at school.   _____

13. I am in the right room.   _____

14. They're in the hall.   _____

15. You're in the classroom.   _____

16. Lynn is in the office.   _____

17. The students are in the library.   _____

18. The teachers are in the staff room.   _____

Practice B   With a partner, put these words into correct English sentences.

1. the / right / am / place / in / I / ?   <u>Am I in the right place?</u>

2. they / students / are / .   <u>They are students.</u>

3. home / at / is / Mary / .   _____

4. aren't / downtown / the / students / .   _____

5. you / the / bathroom / in / are / ?   _____

6. bookstore / are / at / they / the / .   _____

7. Henry / downstairs / are / Mary / and / ?   _____

8. aren't / library / the / in / we / .   _____

9. bookstore / isn't / she / in / the / .   _____

10. hall / the / the / in / teacher / is / .   _____

11. isn't / school / Linda / at / .   _____

12. are / classroom / they / the / in / ?   _____

13. aren't / work / at / you / .   _____

14. the / it / classroom / in / is / ?   _____

15. cafeteria / isn't / the / in / she / .   _____

16. is / the / the / at / bookstore / student / .   _____

17. Lynn / office / the / in / is / ?   _____

18. teachers / the / the / corridor / in / aren't / _____

19. downtown / aren't / students / the / .   _____

Lesson 6   COUNTRY AND NATIONALITY

Explanation

People from **China** are **Chinese**.
People from the **U.S.A.** are **American**.
People from **Japan** are **Japanese**.
People from **Poland** are **Polish**.
People from **Ecuador** are **Ecuadorian**.
People from **Egypt** are **Egyptian**.
People from **Russia** are **Russian**.

People from **Iran** are **Iranian**.
People from **Korea** are **Korean**.
People from **France** are **French**.
People from **Vietnam** are **Vietnamese**.
People from **Peru** are **Peruvian**.
People from **Spain** are **Spanish**.
People from **Italy** are **Italian**.

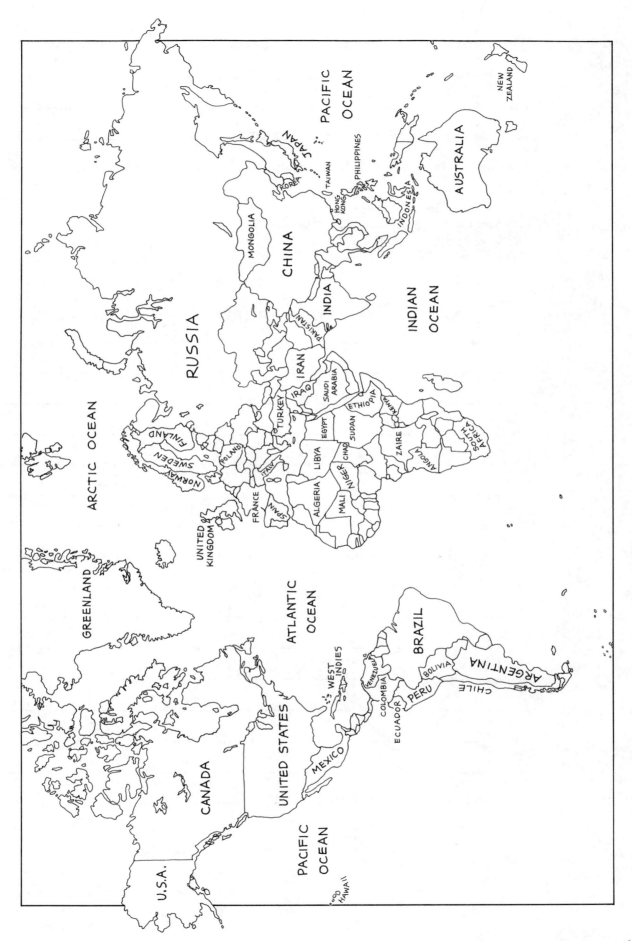

Practice A   Where are you from? _____

What is your nationality? _____

Where is your teacher from? _____

What nationality is your teacher? _____

Stand up. Walk around. Ask all the people in the class these questions:

> Where are you from?
> What is your nationality?

	NAME	COUNTRY	NATIONALITY
1.			
2.			
3.			
4.			
5.			
6.			
7.			
8.			
9.			
10.			
11.			
12.			
13.			
14.			
15.			

Where are most of your classmates from? _____

Practice B   With a partner, match the country and the nationality.

COUNTRY	NATIONALITY
England	Argentinian
Canada	German
Australia	English
America	Canadian
Argentina	American
Germany	Australian
Egypt	Polish
Spain	Brazilian
France	Greek
Greece	French
Brazil	Spanish
Poland	Egyptian

Practice C. Famous People

Work with a partner. Write down the country and nationality of these famous people:

1. Princess Diana __*is*__ from ____*England*____ . ____*She is English.*____ .

2. King Juan Carlos ____ from _____ . _____

3. Prince Charles ____ from _____ . _____

4. Mick Jagger ____ from _____ . _____

5. Wayne Gretzky ____ from _____ . _____

6. Michael Jackson ____ from _____ . _____

7. Pelle ____ from _____ . _____

8. Barbara Streisand ____ from _____ . _____

9. Guillermo Vilas ____ from _____ . _____

11. John Paul II ___ from _____. _____

12. Neil Armstrong ___ from _____. _____

13. Hosni Mubarak ___ from _____. _____

14. Winnie and Nelson Mandela ___ from _____. _____

15. Francois Mitterand ___ from _____. _____

16. Mickey Mouse and Donald Duck ___ from _____. _____

17. My partner ___ from _____. _____

18. I ___ from _____. _____

With your partner, list three famous people and their countries.

     NAME   COUNTRY

1. _____

2. _____

3. _____

Practice D. Famous Places

Work with a partner. Give examples of:

a city _____

a river _____

a mountain _____

a lake _____

a tourist attraction _____

an amusement park _____

Write a statement about these famous places:

1. The White House _____ *is in Washington, D.C. It is an American tourist attraction.* _____

2. Toronto _____ *is in Canada. It is a Canadian city.* _____

3. London _____

4. Melbourne _____

5. The United Nations Building _____

6. Montreal _____

7. The Mississippi _____

8. The Great Wall _____

9. San Diego _____

10. The Grand Canyon _____

11. The Rocky Mountains _____

12. Niagara Falls _____

13. The Statue of Liberty _____

14. The Alps _____

15. The Amazon _____

16. Disneyland _____

17. The Pyramids _____

18. Tokyo _____

List three famous places you know:

1. _____

2. _____

3. _____

Walk around and talk to as many classmates as possible. Ask these questions:

> What is a famous place you know?
> Where is it?

	NAME	PLACE	LOCATION
1.			
2.			
3.			
4.			
5.			
6.			
7.			
8.			
9.			
10.			

Lesson 7 THE VERB *TO BE, WH* QUESTIONS

Explanation   These are some question words:

QUESTION WORD	EXAMPLES	ANSWERS
Who asks about a person.	**Who** is he?	John.
What asks about a thing.	**What** is that?	A pen.
Where asks about a place.	**Where** is she?	At home.
When asks about time.	**When** is the class over?	At 5 o'clock.
Why asks about a reason	**Why** is he at home?	Because he's sick.
How asks about degree.	**How** old are you?	Seventeen.
How asks about manner.	**How** do you get here?	By bus.

Practice A   Answer these questions:

1. Who are you? _____

2. Where are you? _____

3. Where are you from? _____

4. What is your occupation? _____

5. What is your hobby? _____

6. How old are you? _____

7. Where is your school? _____

8. When is your English class? _____

9. Who is your teacher? _____

10. Where are your classmates from? _____

11. How do you come to school? _____

12. Why are you at school? _____

Practice B. Basic Personal Information

Interview two people in your class. Write the information on the chart. The teacher will ask you to report to the class.

QUESTIONS	INFORMATION	PARTNER 1	PARTNER 2
What's your first name?	First name:	_____	_____
What's your surname?	Surname:	_____	_____
_____ ?	Address:	_____	_____
_____ ?	Telephone number:	_____	_____
_____ ?	Age:	_____	_____
_____ ?	Marital status:	_____	_____
_____ ?	Date of birth:	_____	_____
_____ ?	Occupation:	_____	_____
_____ ?	Nationality:	_____	_____
_____ ?	Height:	_____	_____
_____ ?	Weight:	_____	_____
_____ ?	Hobby:	_____	_____

_____ ?   Favorite food: _____   _____

_____ ?   Favorite sport: _____   _____

_____ ?   Favorite color: _____   _____

Practice C   With a partner, make up the questions for these answers.

1. _____*How old are you?*_____ I'm twenty years old.

2. _____? She's in the cafeteria.

3. _____? They're fine.

4. _____? They're erasers.

5. _____? It's a ruler.

6. _____? She's from Colombia.

7. _____? She's seventeen.

8. _____? My hobby is reading.

9. _____? She's at home.

10. _____? That's George.

11. _____? We're in the hall.

12. _____? They're downtown.

13. _____? It's on Saturday night.

14. _____? My birthday is in July.

15. _____? I'm Mary.

16. _____? Because they want to learn.

17. _____? Fine, thanks.

18. _____? They're from Japan.

19. _____? She's a teacher.

20. _____? We're downstairs.

21. _____? It's downtown.

Practice D. To be, **Names, Ages, Occupations**

With a partner, read the stories and answer the questions.

Wendy Reid is from the United States.
She is thirty years old. She is an
English teacher at City College. The
College is in San Diego, California.

What is Wendy's surname? _____

What is her occupation? _____

How old is she? _____

Where is Wendy from? _____

What nationality is Wendy? _____

Bill Jenkins is from Canada. He is forty-two
years old. He is a librarian at York University.
The university is in Toronto, Ontario.

What is Bill's family name? _____

What is his given name? _____

Where is he from? _____

What nationality is Bill? _____

What's Bill's age? _____

Where is York University? _____

3. Melanie and Jim Richards are from the U.S.A. They are both nineteen years old. They are undergraduate students at the State University of New York. The university is in Buffalo, New York.

What is their surname? _____

What are their first names? _____

Where are they from? _____

What are their occupations? _____

How old are they? _____

Where is the university? _____

Write about two people in your class.

1. _____ is from _____.

_____ years old.

_____ at _____.

_____

2. _____ is from _____.

_____ years old.

_____ at _____.

_____

Talk to two people not in your class. Write the information in your notebook. Report to the class.

Practice E   Talk to as many people in the class as possible. Write the information on the chart below. Ask these questions:

> What is your name? Please spell it.
> Where are you from?
> How old are you?
> What is your occupation?

	NAME	COUNTRY	AGE	OCCUPATION
1.				
2.				
3.				
4.				
5.				
6.				
7.				
8.				
9.				
10.				
11.				
12.				
13.				
14.				
15.				

What is the most common occupation of the male students? _____

What is the most common occupation of the female students? _____

Lesson 8 PROPER NAMES AND PRONOUNS

Explanation   It can be difficult to recognize men's and women's first names. You need to pay special attention to English names.

Practice A   This is a list of the most popular names for baby girls in one part of North America in 1990. With a partner, put them in alphabetical order.

GIRLS' NAMES

1. Jessica	6. Ashley	11. Emily	16. Megan	21. Lauren
2. Sarah	7. Nicole	12. Rebecca	17. Alexandra	22. Victoria
3. Stephanie	8. Jennifer	13. Michelle	18. Danielle	23. Courtney
4. Amanda	9. Brittany	14. Laura	19. Rachel	24. Marie
5. Samantha	10. Melissa	15. Kayla	20. Cassandra	25. Lindsay

ALPHABETICAL ORDER

1. _____	6. _____	11. _____	16. _____	21. _____
2. _____	7. _____	12. _____	17. _____	22. _____
3. _____	8. _____	13. _____	18. _____	23. _____
4. _____	9. _____	14. _____	19. _____	24. _____
5. _____	10. _____	15. _____	20. _____	25. _____

What is your favorite girl's name? _____

Which girl's names are the same in your country? _____

Practice B These were the most popular boys' names in one part of North America in 1990. Put them in alphabetical order.

BOYS' NAMES

1. Michael	6. Kyle	11. Jordan	16. Alexander	21. Jonathan
2. Matthew	7. Joshua	12. James	17. Adam	22. Eric
3. Christopher	8. Ryan	13. Nicolas	18. Joseph	23. John
4. Andrew	9. David	14. Tyler	19. Kevin	24. Brandon
5. Daniel	10. Justin	15. Robert	20. Steven	25. Thomas

ALPHABETICAL ORDER

1. _____	6. _____	11. _____	16. _____	21. _____
2. _____	7. _____	12. _____	17. _____	22. _____
3. _____	8. _____	13. _____	18. _____	23. _____
4. _____	9. _____	14. _____	19. _____	24. _____
5. _____	10. _____	15. _____	20. _____	25. _____

What is your favorite boy's name? _____

Which boy's names are the same in your country? _____

Practice C   With a partner, write "he" next to the men's names and "she" next to the women's names.

1. Rachel _____
2. Adam _____
3. Megan _____
4. Victoria _____
5. John _____
6. Ashley _____
7. Samantha _____
8. Barry _____
9. Dawn _____
10. Jay _____
11. Kevin _____
12. Jerry _____
13. Diane _____
14. Kenneth _____
15. Terry _____
16. Maureen _____
17. Penny _____
18. Scott _____
19. Jessica _____
20. Nicole _____
21. Joshua _____
22. Brittany _____
23. Justin _____
24. Rebecca _____
25. Tyler _____
26. Lindsay _____
27. Cassandra _____

28. Danielle _____
29. Alexander _____
30. Eric _____
31. Daniel _____
32. Ashley _____
33. Ruth _____
34. Ross _____
35. Roger _____
36. Doris _____
37. Philip _____
38. Melanie _____
39. Sean _____
40. Allen _____
41. Ellen _____
42. Brian _____
43. Jeff _____
44. Jennifer _____
45. Larry _____
46. Stephanie _____
47. David _____
48. Emily _____
49. Nicolas _____
50. Kayla _____
51. Thomas _____
52. Lauren _____
53. Joseph _____
54. Courtney _____

55. Brandon _____

56. Matthew _____

57. Andrew _____

58. Christopher _____

59. Jason _____

60. Jeremy _____

61. Elaine _____

62. Tim _____

63. Sherry _____

64. Keith _____

65. James _____

66. Douglas _____

67. Michael _____

68. Marian _____

69. Steven _____

70. Grace _____

71. Hazel _____

72. Cindy _____

73. Sarah _____

74. Amanda _____

75. Ryan _____

76. Melissa _____

77. Jordan _____

78. Laura _____

79. Robert _____

80. Heather _____

81. Ian _____

82. Ron _____

Practice D   Work with a partner. Use pronouns in place of the names.

1. Dawn is from San Diego. _____ *She's from San Diego.* _____.

2. Daniel is English. _____ *He's English.* _____.

3. Sherry and Jeremy are students. _____

4. Ian is from Boston. _____

5. Marian is from Phoenix. _____

6. Hazel and I are from Miami. _____

7. Hugh is Australian. _____

8. Kevin is from Pittsburgh. _____

9. Doris and Maureen are from Houston. _____

10. Heather is from Scotland. _____

11. Jeff is Canadian. _____

12. Jennifer is from Philadelphia. _____

13. Larry is Irish. _____

14. Barry and Keith are Canadian. _____

15. Emily and Laura are from Seattle. _____

16. Douglas is from New Zealand. _____

17. Roger and I are from Los Angeles. _____

18. Nicole is from Kansas City. _____

19. Thomas and Rachel are from Atlanta. _____

<table>
<tr><td>Lesson 9</td><td>PRONOUNS AND OCCUPATIONS</td></tr>
</table>

Practice A   With a partner, use the correct pronoun.

1. This is Melissa.

_____ *She's* _____ a doctor.

2. This is Scott and this is Sarah.

_____ *They're* _____ nurses.

3. This is Megan.

_____ a dentist.

4. This is Jordan.

_____ a teacher.

5. This is Robert and this is Thomas.

_____ tellers.

6. This is Brian.

_____ a tailor.

7. This is Emily.

_____ a receptionist.

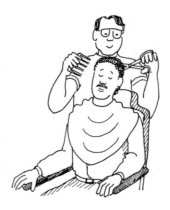

8. This is Larry.

_____ a barber.

9. This is Jessica.

_____ a carpenter.

10. This is Danielle.

_____ a bus driver.

11. This is Kerry and this is Jack.

_____ welders.

12. This is Allan and this is Erica.

_____ plumbers.

13. This is Steven.

_____ a florist.

14. This is David and this is Joshua.

_____ accountants.

15. This is Ross and this is Roger.

_____ bakers.

16. This is Ellen and this is Marie.

_____ waitresses.

Write about your partner.

This is _____.

_____.

Introduce your partner to the class.

Practice B. Pronouns, Occupations, the Verb to be

Explanation Use *he* to replace a man's name.
Use *she* to replace a woman's name.
Use *they* to replace two or more names.
Use *we* to replace *I* and one or more pronouns or names.
With a partner, restate these sentences using the pronouns *he, she, they,* or *we.*

1. Stephanie is a bus driver. _____ *She's a bus driver.* _____

2. Brian is a nurse. _____ *He's a nurse.* _____

3. Ellen and I are musicians. _____ *We're musicians.* _____

4. Ryan is a tailor. _____.

5. Allen and Ron are bakers. _____

6. Adam and I are receptionists. _____

7. Heather is a doctor. _____

8. Justin and David are welders. _____

9. Matthew is a barber. _____

10. Emily and Maureen are tellers. _____

11. Joseph is a carpenter. _____

12. Cindy is a florist. _____

13. Rachel is a secretary. _____

14. Melissa and Grace are accountants. _____

15. Penny is a waitress. _____

16. Danielle and Steven are dentists. _____

17. Allan and I are factory workers. _____

18. Ruth and Nicole are plumbers. _____

19. Amanda and I are nurses. _____

Practice C   Work with a partner. Use the correct form of the verb to be in these sentences.

1. I ___*am*___ from Canada.

2. Where ___*are*___ you from?

3. Justin (negative) ___*isn't*___ a teller.

4. He _____ a student.

5. _____ you a teacher?

6. What _____ your name?

7. How old _____ you?

8. What _____ your occupation?

9. Where _____ the school?

10. I (negative) _____ at home.

11. She (negative) _____ a nurse.

12. _____ it downtown?

13. How tall _____ you?

14. Why _____ they here?

15. They _____ from France.

16. You _____ from North America.

17. We (negative) _____ in the classroom.

18. The waitresses _____ in the kitchen.

19. The plumber _____ in the basement.

20. I _____ from Poland.

21. Brian and Jessica _____ at the hospital.

22. Who _____ in the office?

23. Emily (negative) _____ at the bookstore.

24. They (negative) _____ in the library.

Practice D   With a partner, read this story and use the correct form of the verb *to be* in the blanks.

Attendance in the English Class

It _____ 9:30, and there _____ only five students in our class this morning. Laura (negative) _____ here. She _____ late every morning. Michael and Sarah _____ away today because they _____ sick. Marie (negative) _____ very well either. She _____ at the doctor's office this morning. Kevin and Emily (negative) _____ here because their friends from Chicago _____ in town this week. Daniel (negative) _____ here. He _____ at the dentist's. Jessica _____ also absent. She _____ at the student employment office. Diane _____ at the counsellor's office. Rachel _____ probably in the cafeteria. Ryan and Douglas _____ at work this morning. Even the regular teacher _____ not in today. She _____ at a teacher's meeting. I certainly hope everyone _____ here tomorrow!

With a partner, write about your class. Write about the people who are absent and where you think they are. Write about the people who are present, too.

Explanation   It's important to tell the difference between a first name and a surname. Some names, such as Scott or Charles, can be a first name or a last name.

Practice A   Work with a partner. Organize the names below into these categories.

WOMEN'S FIRST NAMES	MEN'S FIRST NAMES	SURNAMES

John	Wood	Scott	Matthews
Josephson	McDonald	Adams	Cooper
Ryan	Andrews	Ashley	Stevens
Jennifer	Allen	Jones	David
Michael	Laura	Peters	Susan
Donald	Armstrong	Clark	Gibson
Bush	Cunningham	Davies	Eaton
Fred	Eric	Fitzpatrick	Hughes
Roberts	Rachel	King	Hunter
Jordan	Michelle	Thomas	Spencer
Taylor	Kevin	Kelly	Richardson

Practice B   This is a game. Work with a group. Try to make up as many English names as possible. Both the first name and the last name must begin with the same letter of the alphabet.

Examples: Anne Anderson, Brian Brown, etc.

ENGLISH NAMES

1. _____   5. _____   9. _____

2. _____   6. _____   10. _____

3. _____   7. _____   11. _____

4. _____   8. _____   12. _____

13. _____   18. _____   23. _____

14. _____   19. _____   24. _____

15. _____   20. _____   25. _____

16. _____   21. _____   26. _____

17. _____   22. _____

Lesson 11 | TIME

Explanation

What time is it?
It's eight o'clock.

What time is it?
It's three o'clock.

What time is it?
It's six o'clock.

What's the time?
It's twelve-thirty.
It's half past twelve.

What's the time?
It's three-thirty.
It's half past three.

What's the time?
It's five-thirty.
It's half past five.

What time is it?
It's a quarter to nine.
It's fifteen to nine.

What time is it?
It's five to nine.
It's five before nine.

What time is it?
It's twenty-five to nine.
It's twenty-five before nine.

What's the time?	What's the time?	What's the time?
It's a quarter after three.	It's five after three.	It's twenty-five after three.
It's fifteen past three.	It's five past three.	It's twenty-five past three.

American English uses A.M. for the time between midnight and noon, and P.M. for the time between noon and midnight.

Practice A   With a partner, draw the times on these clocks.

| 1. What time is it? | 2. What's the time? | 3. What time is it? |
| It's nine o'clock. | It's eight-thirty. | It's a quarter past two. |

| 4. What's the time? | 5. What time is it? | 6. What's the time? |
| It's a quarter to one. | It's half past twelve. | It's twenty after six. |

7. _____?   8. _____?   9. _____?
It's a quarter past three.   It's five after five.   It's ten to ten.

10._____?   11. _____?   12. _____?

It's a quarter to nine.   It's twenty past twelve.   It's five to six.

What are some different ways to ask for the time?

_____?

_____?

Practice B   With a partner, write out these times:

7:05 _____   _____

6:30 _____   _____

12:00 _____   _____

11:20 _____   _____

5:45 _____   _____

3:30 _____   _____

4:15 _____   _____

2:45 _____   _____

9:40 _____   _____

10:50 _____   _____

8:10 _____   _____

3:15 _____   _____

5:55 _____   _____

Answer these questions about your everyday schedule:

What time do you get up? _____

What time do you go to bed? _____

What time do you start your English class? _____

What time do you finish your English class? _____

What time do you eat your breakfast? _____

What time do you eat your lunch? _____

What time do you eat your supper? _____

Lesson 12 ORDINAL NUMBERS

Explanation

1st	2nd	3rd	4th	5th	6th	7th	8th	9th
first	second	third	fourth	fifth	sixth	seventh	eighth	ninth

10th	11th	12th	13th	14th	15th	20th
tenth	eleventh	twelfth	thirteenth	fourteenth	fifteenth	twentieth

21st	22nd	23rd	24th
twenty-first	twenty-second	twenty-third	twenty-fourth

30th	40th	50th	100th
thirtieth	fortieth	fiftieth	one hundredth

101st	1000th
one hundred and first	one thousandth

We use ordinal numbers to show the order of things.

Examples: my first love, my first job, my second car, the fifth floor, the twenty-second floor

We use ordinal numbers for dates.

Examples: 8/21st/94: the twenty-first of August nineteen ninety-four

1/30th/95: the thirtieth of January, nineteen ninety-five

Practice A   With a partner write out these ordinal numbers.

16th _____	25th _____	60th _____
17th _____	31st _____	70th _____
18th _____	32nd _____	80th _____
19th _____	33rd _____	90th _____
45th _____	56th _____	91st _____
102nd _____	103rd _____	99th _____

These are the months of the year in English:

January	May	September
February	June	October
March	July	November
April	August	December

These are the days of the week in English:

Monday	Thursday	Sunday
Tuesday	Friday	
Wednesday	Saturday	

Practice A   With a partner, write out the full names for the abbreviations.

Apr. _____   Tues. _____

Feb. _____   Fri. _____

Aug. _____   Sat. _____

Sept. _____   Mon. _____

Jan. _____   Wed. _____

Nov. _____   Thurs. _____

Mar. _____   Sun. _____

Dec. _____

Oct. _____

Practice B   With your partner, write out and say these expiration dates.

Best before 7/13/93: _____

Best before 12/30/96: _____

Best before 11/15/95: _____

Best before 10/23/94: _____

Best before 9/27/95: _____

Best before 6/21/96: _____

Best before 2/12/94: _____

Best before 1/8/95: _____

```
                    INFORMATION
  OCCUPANT                              SUITE

  Barry's Barber Shop.....................105
  Denture Clinic.........................201
  Dr. S. Eaton, Dentist..................1230
  The Exclusive Tailor...................414
  The Eye Clinic.........................1001
  J. Jones, Accountant...................501
  Dr. Samuel Lee, Family Practice.......1115
  Love's Florists........................313
```

Practice C   With your partner, read the information board and answer these questions.

What floor is the denture clinic on? _____

What floor is the flower shop on? _____

Where is the accountant's office? _____

Where is the dentist's office? _____

What floor is the barber shop on? _____

Where is the doctor's office? _____

What floor is the eye clinic on? _____

Where is the tailor's shop? _____

Practice D   Walk around and talk to as many people as possible. Ask these questions:

> What is your name? Please spell it.
> When is your birthday?
> What sign are you?

ASTROLOGICAL SIGNS

Aries
(Mar. 21–Apr. 19)

Taurus
(Apr. 20–May 20)

Gemini
(May 21–June 21)

Cancer
(June 21–July 22)

Leo
(July 23–Aug. 22)

Virgo
(Aug. 23–Sept. 22)

Libra
(Sept. 23–Oct. 23)

Scorpio
(Oct. 24–Nov. 21)

Sagittarius
(Nov. 22–Dec. 21)

Capricorn
(Dec. 22–Jan. 19)

Aquarius
(Jan. 20–Feb. 18)

Pisces
(Feb. 19–Mar. 20)

	NAME	BIRTHDAY	SIGN
1.			
2.			
3.			
4.			
5.			
6.			
7.			
8.			
9.			
10.			
11.			
12.			
13.			
14.			
15.			

Are there any students who have the same birthday? _____

With a partner, write out the names of the months in each season.

SEASONS	MONTHS
	_____
winter	_____
	_____

	_____
spring	_____
	_____

	_____
summer	_____
	_____

	_____
fall	_____
	_____

Practice A   Match the holiday with the date or season. If you or your partner don't know a holiday, ask someone outside your class to help you.

Christmas	Jan. 1st
Valentine's Day	Oct. 31st
Labor Day	spring
Thanksgiving Day	Dec. 25th
Easter	fall
New Year's Day	September
Halloween	Feb. 14th
April Fool's Day	May
Groundhog Day	Apr. 1st
American Independence Day	February
Mother's Day	July 4th

Write about three holidays.

Example: Christmas is in December. Christmas is on December 25th.

1. _____

2. _____

3. _____

Practice B   Walk around. Talk to as many people as possible. Ask these questions:

> What's your name? Please spell it.
> What's your favorite season?
> What's your favorite holiday?

	NAME	FAVORITE SEASON	FAVORITE HOLIDAY
1.			
2.			
3.			
4.			
5.			
6.			
7.			
8.			
9.			
10.			
11.			

12. _____		
13. _____		
14. _____		
15. _____		

What's the most popular holiday? _____

Practice C. Holidays Around the World

Think of an important holiday in your country. _____

When is it? _____

Walk around. Talk to your classmates. Ask these questions:

> What is an important holiday in your country?
> When is it?

List as many holidays as you can on the chart. The teacher will ask you to report to the class.

JANUARY	FEBRUARY	MARCH
_____	_____	_____
_____	_____	_____
_____	_____	_____

APRIL	MAY	JUNE
_____	_____	_____
_____	_____	_____
_____	_____	_____

JULY	AUGUST	SEPTEMBER
_____	_____	_____
_____	_____	_____
_____	_____	_____

OCTOBER	NOVEMBER	DECEMBER
_____	_____	_____
_____	_____	_____
_____	_____	_____

Practice D   With a partner, read this notice and then answer the questions.

```
                    Metropolitan Library
                           Hours
   Mon. to Thurs.          9 A.M. to 9 P.M.
                           (to 8 P.M. July/Aug.)
   Fri.                    9 A.M. to 6 P.M.
   Sat.                    10 A.M. to 5 P.M.
   Sun.                    1:30 to 5 P.M. (closed Sun. May to Labor Day)
   Audiovisual Department:  5th floor
   Mon. to Sat.            regular library hours
   Sun.                    closed

                     Holiday Closings
   Christmas Day          Good Friday        Independence Day
   New Year's Day         Easter Sunday      Labor Day
   Martin Luther King Day Easter Monday      Thanksgiving Day
```

Write "true" or "false" after each statement.

1. The library is open on Saturdays.   _____**true**_____

2. The library is closed at Easter.   _____

3. The library is open at 9 A.M. every day.   _____

4. The library is closed on Dec. 25th.   _____

5. The library is closed on July 4th.   _____

6. The A. V. Department is open every day.   _____

7. The library is open every Sunday.   _____

8. The library is open until 9 P.M. every night.   _____

9. The library closes early on Saturdays.   _____

10. The library has short hours every Sunday.   _____

11. The library is closed on Thanksgiving day.   _____

12. The library is open on Jan. 1st.   _____

Explanation   We spell the plural forms of regular nouns with *s* or *es*.

SINGULAR	PLURAL
1 chair	13 chairs
1 desk	30 desks
1 watch	15 watches

A small number of nouns are not regular.

SINGULAR	PLURAL
1 man	14 men
1 woman	16 women
1 child	40 children
1 tooth	18 teeth
1 foot	2 feet
1 mouse	19 mice
1 knife	17 knives

Pronunciation Note   We pronounce the regular plural in three different ways.

1. Pronounce the plural as *iz* when the noun ends in a sound like *s* (a sibilant).

Examples: faces   dresses   brushes   churches   buses   mixes

2. Pronounce the plural as *z* when the noun finishes with a sound that vibrates in your throat (a voiced sound).

Examples: pens   bags   boys   girls   fingers   hands   windows   cabs

3. Pronounce the plural as *s* when the noun ends in a consonant sound that doesn't vibrate in your throat (a voiceless consonant).

Examples: books   cups   hats   forks   plates   lips

Practice A   Work with a small group. Put all the nouns with the same plural sounds together.

KITCHEN THINGS	LIVING ROOM THINGS	OFFICE THINGS
plates	rugs	desks
glasses	lamps	pens
forks	couches	books
stoves	armchairs	folders
ovens	tables	computers
cupboards	televisions	typewriters
fridges	cushions	copiers
spoons	drapes	staplers
faucets	loveseats	filing cabinets
dishes	bookcases	paper clips
sinks	clocks	binders
place mats	mirrors	rulers

Plural sounds like *z*	Plural sounds like *s*	Plural sounds like *es*
_____	_____	_____
_____	_____	_____
_____	_____	_____
_____	_____	_____
_____	_____	_____
_____	_____	_____
_____	_____	_____
_____	_____	_____
_____	_____	_____

Practice B   Work with a partner. Check each other's work. Make the subject nouns plural.

1. The pen is in the drawer. _____ *The pens are in the drawer.* _____

2. The computer is in the library. _____

3. Is the typewriter in the office? _____

4. The filing cabinet isn't open. _____

5. The pencil sharpener is on the desk. _____

6. The stapler isn't in the library. _____

7. Is the paper clip in the box? _____

8. The dish isn't in the sink. _____

9. Is the plate in the cupboard? _____

10. The spoon isn't in the drawer. _____

11. The fork isn't clean. _____

12. Is the glass dirty? _____

13. The cushion is on the couch. _____

14. Is the lamp in the living room? _____

15. The mirror isn't broken. _____

16. Is the television set out of order? _____

17. The clock is slow. _____

18. The man is in the kitchen. _____

19. The child is outside. _____

20. The woman is upstairs. _____

21. My foot is sore. _____

22. The dish is on the counter. _____

Lesson 16 | PREPOSITIONS

Explanation Prepositions show place. Here are some prepositions:

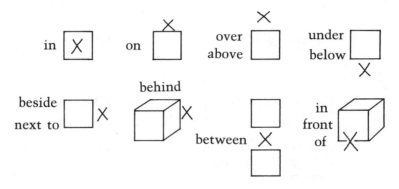

Practice A With a partner, read about the living room. Then look at the picture and use prepositions and the verb *to be* in the sentences.

The Living Room

The furniture is in the living room. The rug is on the floor. The lamp is beside the sofa. The coffee table is in front of the sofa. The end table is between the sofa and the chair. The mirror is over the television set. The rug is under the coffee table. The picture window is behind the sofa. The electrical outlets are on the wall behind the sofa.

1. The coffee table _____*is on*_____ the rug.

2. The flowers _____ the vase.

3. The television set _____ the mirror.

4. The armchair _____ the sofa.

5. The vase _____ the end table.

6. The lamp _____ the window.

7. The electrical outlet _____ the sofa.

8. The cushions _____ the sofa.

9. The curtains _____ the window.

10. The coffee table _____ the sofa.

11. The end table _____ the armchair.

12. The sofa _____ the window.

13. The news program _____ T.V.

Practice B   Describe your living room. Make three statements about your living room. Use prepositions. Then get the same information from your partner.
Ask your partner:

   What's in your living room?
   Where is it?

MY LIVING ROOM   MY PARTNER'S LIVING ROOM

1. _____   _____

2. _____   _____

3. _____   _____

Practice C   With a partner, read about the kitchen. Then look at the picture and use prepositions and the correct form of the verb *to be* in the sentences.

The Kitchen

This kitchen is modern and easy to work in. The refrigerator is next to the cupboards. The counter is next to the stove. The microwave oven is above the stove. The sink is below the window. The garbage can is in the lower cupboard under the sink. The dishes are in the upper cupboards. The cups are in the sink. The groceries are on the counter. There is a round table in the middle of the room. The light fixture is over the table. The chairs are beside the table. Nefertiti, the friendly cat, is always under the table.

1. The stove ___*is beside*___ the sink.

2. The window _____ the sink.

3. The groceries _____ the counter.

4. The glasses _____ the cupboard.

5. The plates _____ the cupboard.

6. The bowls _____ the cupboard.

7. The garbage can _____ the sink.

8. The kitchen table _____ the light fixture.

9. The cups _____ the sink.

10. The bags of groceries _____ the fridge.

11. The cat _____ the table.

12. The stove _____ the microwave oven.

13. The food _____ the fridge.

14. The kitchen counter _____ the stove and the refrigerator.

Describe your kitchen. Use prepositions. Then get the same information from your partner. Ask your partner:

> What's your kitchen like?
> What's in your kitchen?
> Where is it?

MY KITCHEN	MY PARTNER'S KITCHEN
1. _____	_____
2. _____	_____
3. _____	_____
4. _____	_____

Practice D. Bedroom Furniture

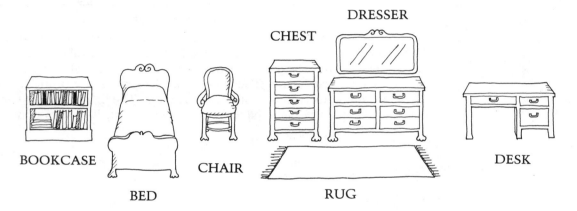

BOOKCASE   BED   CHAIR   CHEST   DRESSER   RUG   DESK

Draw a picture of your bedroom. Write three things about your bedroom. Use prepositions.

MY BEDROOM

1. _____

2. _____

3. _____

Tell your partner about your bedroom. Your partner will draw a picture of your bedroom. Then draw a picture of your partner's bedroom. What's your partner's bedroom like?

MY PARTNER'S BEDROOM

1. _____

2. _____

3. _____

Practice E   Work with a partner. Use the verb *to be* and a correct preposition. Check each other's work.

1. The sofa _____is in_____ the living room.

2. The flowers _____are in_____ the vase.

3. The window _____ the sofa.

4. The electical outlets _____ the wall.

5. _____ the mirror _____ the T.V. set?

6. _____ the chair _____ the sofa?

7. The children (negative) _____ the living room.

8. The men _____ the kitchen.

9. _____ the dishes _____ the cupboard?

10. The vegetables _____ the fridge.

11. The spoons (negative) _____ the table.

12. The knives and forks _____ the drawer.

13. _____ the dresser _____ the bed?

14. The desk _____ the window.

15. The rug _____ the bed.

16. _____ the chest _____ the door?

17. The glasses _____ the table.

18. I (negative) _____ the bedroom.

19. We _____ the family room.

20. He (negative) _____ the bathroom.

21. The women _____ the living room.

22. _____ you _____ the kitchen?

23. They _____ the basement.

24. It (negative) _____ the fridge.

Lesson 17 | DIRECT COMMANDS

Explanation It is important to follow basic instructions, in writing or in speaking. These instructions are often direct commands.

Examples:

Write your name.
Sign this paper.

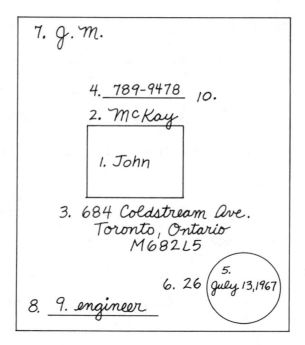

Look at the instructions. See how we follow the instructions.

1. Print your first name in the box.

2. Write your surname above the box.

3. Write your address under the box.

4. Write your phone number above your surname.

5. Write your date of birth in the circle in the lower right corner.

6. Write your age beside the circle.

7. Write your initials in the upper left corner.

8. Draw a line at the bottom of the page.

9. Write your occupation on the line.

10. Underline your telephone number.

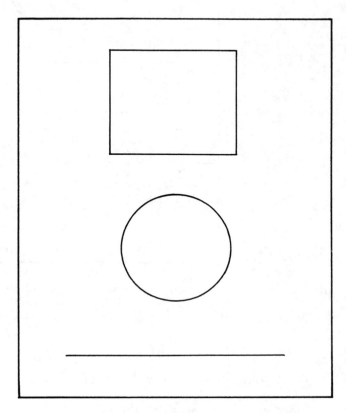

Practice A   Give these instructions to your partner. Your partner will then give you instructions.

1. Write your first name above the circle.

2. Print your surname under the circle.

3. Write your address in the circle.

4. Write your occupation in the box at the top of the page.

5. Write your telephone number beside the box.

6. Sign your name on the line at the bottom.

7. Write your initials under the line.

8. Write your date of birth in the top right corner.

Compare your answers. How many mistakes do you have? _____

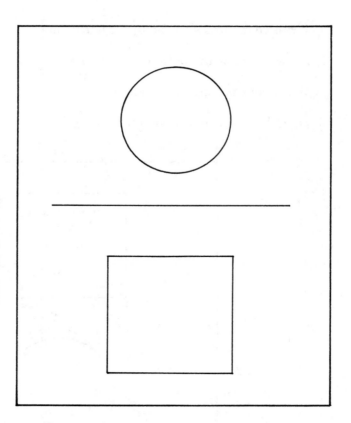

Practice B   Give these instructions to your partner. Then follow your partner's instructions.

1. Write your full name in the circle.

2. Write your address in the box.

3. Write your telephone number under the box.

4. Write your surname above the circle.

5. Print your first name on the line.

6. Write your occupation beside your surname.

7. Write your date of birth under the line.

8. Write your age in the lower right corner.

9. Write your initials in the upper left corner.

Number of mistakes? _____

dress

blouse

pullover

jeans

socks

vest

purse

shorts

undershirt

slippers

shoes

bathing suit

jacket

belt

sweatshirt

gloves

suspenders

coat

pants

shirt

sundress

teeshirt

mittens

bracelet

trenchcoat

skirt

sweater

cowboy boots

hat

pantyhose

suit

long underwear

scarf

earrings

necklace

tie

Practice A   Work with a partner. Look at the words for clothes. Write "male" next to the men's clothes and "female" next to the women's clothes. If the clothing is for both men and women, write "unisex."

dress _____   suit _____

tie _____   purse _____

jacket _____   shirt _____

skirt _____   long underwear _____

blouse _____   shorts _____

belt _____   sun dress _____

sweater _____   scarf _____

pullover _____   undershirt _____

sweatshirt _____   teeshirt _____

cowboy boots _____ slippers _____

gloves _____   mittens _____

hat _____   earrings _____

jeans _____   shoes _____

suspenders _____   bracelet _____

pantyhose _____   necklace _____

socks _____   bathing suit _____

coat _____   trench coat _____

vest _____   pants _____

Circle the words for the clothes each of you has on. Report to the class.

Explanation Pronouns and proper nouns (names) have possessive forms.

SUBJECT PRONOUN	POSSESSIVE ADJECTIVE
I	my
you	your
he	his
she	her
it	its
we	our
they	their

PROPER NOUN	POSSESSIVE FORM
Jack	Jack's
Mary	Mary's
Charles	Charles'
Fred and Sharon	Fred's and Sharon's

Examples:

PRONOUN	POSSESSIVE
I have a new coat.	**My** new coat is warm.
You have a new jacket.	**Your** new jacket is stylish.
He has a new hat.	**His** new hat is very nice.
Jack has a new tie.	**Jack's** new tie is bright.
She has a new raincoat.	**Her** new raincoat is long.
Mary has new boots.	**Mary's** new boots are fashionable.
It has a new collar.	**Its** new collar is pretty.
We have new sweaters.	**Our** new sweaters are warm.
They have new gloves.	**Their** new gloves are expensive.
Fred and Sharon have new belts.	**Fred's and Sharon's** new belts are nice.

Explanation We put the color word before the noun or after the verb *to be*.

Examples:

My **black** coat is new.
My new coat is **black.**

Here are some colors in English:

black	yellow
white	orange
blue	red
green	purple
grey	pink
beige	violet

Practice A With a partner, read the description of Wendy and answer the questions about her clothes.

Wendy Reid has a skirt and jacket on today. Wendy's black skirt is short. Her yellow jacket is long. Wendy's blouse is black and white. Her belt and scarf are grey. Her shoes and stockings are black. Wendy's purse is grey. She looks very nice.

What's black and white? _____

What's grey? _____

What's yellow? _____

What's black? _____

Describe your clothes. Get the same information from your partner. Report to the class.

	MY CLOTHES	MY PARTNER'S CLOTHES
1.	_____	_____
2.	_____	_____
3.	_____	_____

Practice B With a partner, use the information below to make statements with possessives and colors.

1. Mary Ann, coat, new, black. _____ *Mary Ann's new coat is black.*

2. they, gloves, brown, warm. _____ *Their brown gloves are warm.*

3. we, socks, new, yellow. _____

4. you, pants, grey, stylish. _____

5. George, belt, red, leather. _____

6. Jason, sweater, old, purple. _____

7. Jessica, skirt, green, long. _____

8. I, jeans, light blue, fashionable. _____

9. Bob and Linda, shoes, new, beige. _____

10. Stephanie, dress, pink, nice. _____

11. Ann, boots, winter, brown. _____

12. she, purse, white, leather. _____

13. he, shirt, new, blue. _____

14. they, jackets, red, nice. _____

15. you, pullover, yellow, attractive. _____

16. she, slippers, old, grey. _____

17. we, coats, spring, dark blue. _____

18. the children, sweatshirts, new, grey. _____

19. he, hat, green, attractive. _____

20. I, umbrella, red, old. _____

Write about two classmates who have something new on.

1. _____

2. _____

Lesson 20	DESCRIBING PEOPLE

Explanation   Here are some adjectives to describe people:

HEIGHT	WEIGHT	HAIR
tall	heavy	long
short	thin	short
of medium height	of medium build	curly
		straight
		blonde
		brown
		black
		red
		grey

EYES	PERSONALITY	CLOTHES
big	friendly	nice
blue	nice	stylish
brown	happy	casual
green	quiet	expensive
grey	talkative	neat

Practice A   Work with a partner. Describe each other.

	ME	MY PARTNER
Hair color:		
Eye color:		
Height:		
Weight:		
Other:		

Write a description of your partner.

_____

_____

_____

_____

Practice B   Work with a partner. Use possessive adjectives to replace the names in these sentences.

1. John's hair is long. _____ *His hair is long.* _____

2. Cassandra's eyes are grey. _____ *Her eyes are grey.* _____

3. Lauren's clothes are expensive. _____

4. Jennifer's hair is curly. _____

5. Steven's and Andrew's clothes are stylish. _____

6. Ellen's hair is straight. _____

7. Maureen's hair is red. _____

8. Cindy's and Joseph's smiles are friendly. _____

9. Sam's clothes are casual. _____

10. Christopher's voice is loud and clear. _____

11. Jane's and John's clothes are expensive. _____

12. Steven's voice is deep. _____

13. Linda's watch and my watch are cheap. _____

14. Susan's and Marsha's scarves are long. _____

Lesson 21 ADJECTIVES

Explanation   Adjectives describe or give information about people or things. We put adjectives before the noun.

Examples:

The **tall** man is here.
The **new** books are in the library.

We can put adjectives at the end of a sentence if they come after a verb such as *to be*.

Examples:

The man is **tall.**
The books in the library are **new.**

Practice A   Work with a partner. Put a check mark (√) next to the adjectives that describe each of you.

	ME	MY PARTNER
tall	_____	_____
short	_____	_____
strong	_____	_____
neat	_____	_____
heavy	_____	_____
thin	_____	_____
of medium build	_____	_____
pretty	_____	_____
handsome	_____	_____
rich	_____	_____
poor	_____	_____
shy	_____	_____
happy	_____	_____
sad	_____	_____
quiet	_____	_____
talkative	_____	_____
noisy	_____	_____

busy	_____	_____
friendly	_____	_____
lazy	_____	_____

Write three things about you.

1. _____

2. _____

3. _____

Write three things about your partner.

1. _____

2. _____

3. _____

Report two things that are the same about both of you:

1. _____

2. _____

Practice B Look at the list of adjectives and put a check mark next to the words that tell about the place you live now and the place you lived before.

	THIS CITY	LAST CITY
old	_____	_____
new	_____	_____
big	_____	_____
small	_____	_____
rich	_____	_____
poor	_____	_____
modern	_____	_____
clean	_____	_____
dirty	_____	_____
crowded	_____	_____
safe	_____	_____
dangerous	_____	_____

quiet   _____   _____

noisy   _____   _____

busy   _____   _____

beautiful   _____   _____

ugly   _____   _____

friendly   _____   _____

unfriendly   _____   _____

Write three things about this city:

1. _____

2. _____

3. _____

Write three things about your last city:

1. _____

2. _____

3. _____

Work with a partner. Write down and report three things you both think about this city.

1. _____

2. _____

3. _____

Write down and report two interesting things about your partner's last city.

1. _____

2. _____

Practice C   Work with a partner. Rewrite these sentences with the opposites of the adjectives.

1. Jets aren't slow. _____ *They're fast.* _____

2. The Empire State Building is high. _____ *It isn't low.* _____

3. The U.S.A. isn't an old country. _____

4. New York isn't a small city. _____

5. The city hall is a modern building. _____

6. The park isn't noisy. _____

7. The streets downtown are clean. _____

8. Most students aren't rich. _____

9. The buses and streetcars aren't fast. _____

10. This city isn't dangerous. _____

11. Ellen and I are old. _____

12. Diane and Jeff aren't thin. _____

13. The furniture isn't light. _____

14. The dishes are cheap. _____

15. Emily is friendly. _____

16. Maureen and I aren't busy. _____

17. Ryan isn't noisy. _____

18. Larry is healthy. _____

19. The book isn't interesting. _____

20. Rebecca and Penny aren't short. _____

21. The music isn't loud. _____

22. The couch isn't soft. _____

23. The lake is shallow. _____

24. The factory isn't pretty. _____

25. The colors aren't dark. _____

26. The rug isn't thin. _____

Describe your school. _____

Describe your apartment. _____

Describe your best friend. _____

Describe your teacher. _____

Explanation   We use *there* in sentences to say that something exists. *There* has no special meaning. Its job is to be the subject of the sentence.

Examples:

There's a hardware store on College Street.
There are some cars in the parking lot.
Is there a drinking fountain in the hall?
Are there any students in the classroom?
There isn't a bakery on this street.
There aren't any banks in this plaza.

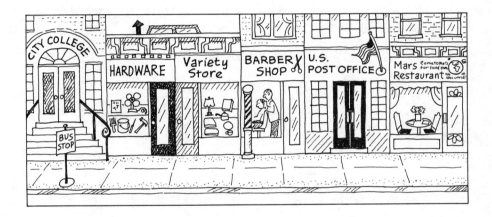

Practice A. City College

With a partner, read about City College and answer the questions.

City College is located at 506 Coronado Drive. It is near downtown San Diego. It's in a very busy neighborhood. Across the street from the college there is a bank. Next to the bank there's a church. There is a bus stop in front of the college and a large parking lot behind the building. Next door to the college there is a hardware store. Beside the hardware store there is a variety store. There's a barber shop next to the variety store. There's a post office beside that. There aren't any grocery stores nearby, but there are several restaurants and cafes in the neighborhood.

There are many office buildings and department stores within walking distance of the college. Some of the city's hospitals are just around the corner. But the best thing of all is that the ocean and the beaches are just a short drive down the street.

1. Where is City College? _____ *It is at 506 Coronado Drive.* _____

2. Which neighborhood is the college in? _____ *It's downtown.* _____

3. Is there a bus stop nearby? _____ *Yes, there is. There's a bus stop in front of the college.*

4. Is there a bank nearby? _____

5. Is there a parking lot nearby? _____

6. Is there a hardware store in the neighborhood? _____

7. Is there a post office in the area? _____

8. Is there a drugstore nearby? _____

9. Is there a coffee shop in the area? _____

10. Are there any department stores nearby? _____

11. Is there a hospital in the area? _____

12. Are there any grocery stores nearby? _____

13. What else is close to the college? _____

Practice B   Write four things about your neighborhood. Then ask your partner about his or her neighborhood.

MY NEIGHBORHOOD	MY PARTNER'S NEIGHBORHOOD
1. _____	_____
2. _____	_____
3. _____	_____
4. _____	_____

What is the same about your neighborhoods?

_____

_____

Practice C   Talk to your partner. Put a check mark (√) next to those things your school has, and an (X) next to those your school doesn't have.

	WE HAVE	WE DON'T HAVE
telephones	_____	_____
a cafeteria	_____	_____
a library	_____	_____
a ladies' room	_____	_____
a men's room	_____	_____
a coffee machine	_____	_____
a computer lab	_____	_____
an emergency exit	_____	_____
a pencil sharpener	_____	_____

a registration office   _____   _____

a language lab   _____   _____

a gym or fitness center   _____   _____

a daycare center   _____   _____

a nurse's office   _____   _____

a students' lounge   _____   _____

a counsellor's office   _____   _____

a swimming pool   _____   _____

an elevator   _____   _____

a parking lot   _____   _____

With your partner, add some others:

1. _____

2. _____

Write four things about your school.

Example: There are telephones on the first floor, near the exit.

1. _____

2. _____

3. _____

4. _____

Practice D   With a partner, answer these questions about your school

1. Excuse me, where is the ladies' room? _*There's a ladies' room on the second floor.*_

2. Excuse me, is there a cigarette machine here? _*I'm sorry, there isn't a cigarette*_ _*machine in this building.*_

3. Excuse me, where is the library? _____

4. Excuse me, are there any elevators here? _____

5. Excuse me, where is the men's room? _____

6. Excuse me, is there a gym here? _____

7. Excuse me, where is the photocopier? _____

8. Excuse me, is there a cafeteria in this building? _____

9. Excuse me, where are the public phones? _____

10. Excuse me, are there any computers here? _____

11. Excuse me, where is the students' parking lot? _____

12. Excuse me, are there any tape recorders here? _____

13. Excuse me, where is the pencil sharpener? _____

You and your partner ask some questions now.

14. _____

15. _____

16. _____

Then find another pair of students to answer the questions.

Lesson 23 REVIEW: THE VERB *TO BE*

Explanation of Short Answers Here are some short answers to questions:

Are you single	**Yes, I am.**
Is Adam from a country in Europe?	**No, he isn't.**
Are they tired?	**Yes, they are.**

Practice A Walk around. Talk to your classmates. When you find someone who fits the description in the question, write the person's name. Try to get as many different names as possible.

Example:

> A: Are you single?
> B: Yes, I am.
> A. What's your name? Please spell it.

Find someone in your class who:

is single. _____

is from a country in Europe. _____

is from a country in Asia. _____

isn't rich. _____

is tired. _____

is hungry. _____

isn't happy to be here. _____

is thirsty. _____

isn't shy. _____

is in his or her twenties. _____

isn't worried about exams. _____

is strong. _____

is talkative. _____

is happy today. _____

is busy every evening. _____

isn't lonely. _____

is an employee. _____

is a sports fan. _____

is a country music fan. _____

is a good cook. _____

is a good dancer. _____

Practice B   With a partner, use the correct form of the verb *to be* in this story.

Mars Restaurant

The English students' favorite restaurant _____ called Mars. It _____ downtown on a street

close to City College. Mars _____ famous for its delicious food. The sandwiches _____

thick. The bread _____ very fresh. The soups _____ homemade. The pies, cakes, and

desserts _____ especially good. In fact, all the food _____ wonderful.

The owner of the restaurant _____ also the cook. He _____ a very popular person. He _____

friendly, but always very busy. Mars _____ a noisy place. It _____ always full. Many people

_____ regular customers. They _____ very happy and loyal.

The slogan of the restaurant _____: "Come to Mars—The food _____ out of this world."

Practice C   With a partner, make these statements into questions:

The English Class

1. The new students are shy. _____*Are the new students shy?*_____.

2. The course director is very helpful. _____

3. She's in the office now. _____

4. The English classes are free. _____

5. The teachers are very experienced. _____

6. The classrooms are on the third floor. _____

7. The English secretary is friendly. _____

8. He's available to answer questions. _____

9. The clerks in the registation office are busy. _____

10. Those students are here for registration. _____

11. They're science students. _____

12. We're late for class again. _____

With a partner, make these statements negative.

The City

1. This city is very clean. _____*This city isn't very clean.*_____

2. The streets are very quiet. _____

3. The buildings downtown are old. _____

4. The streets downtown are dangerous. _____

5. Public transportation is expensive. _____

6. The shopping malls are small. _____

7. The people here are rude. _____

8. I'm lonely in this city. _____

9. We're sad here. _____

10. They're bored in the city. _____

Explanation English possessives have three forms.

POSSESSIVE NOUN	POSSESSIVE ADJECTIVE	POSSESSIVE PRONOUN
Mary's	her	hers
John's	his	his
the Smiths'	their	theirs
	my	mine
	your	yours
	our	ours

We don't put the **possessive pronoun** before the noun because its meaning includes the noun.

Examples:

This is **Mary's** car. This car is **Mary's.**
These are **your** gloves. These gloves are **yours.**
That's **my** hat. That hat is **mine.**

Practice A Work with a partner. Use possessive pronouns in these sentences.

1. This is our tape recorder. _____ *This tape recorder is ours.* _____

2. These are his books. _____

3. This is his eraser. _____

4. That's our tape. _____

5. That's their pencil sharpener. _____

6. This is her stapler. _____

7. That's our glue. _____

8. This is your ruler. _____

9. These are your paper clips. _____

10. That's their photocopier. _____

11. This is your file folder. _____

12. That's her filing cabinet. _____

13. This is my desk. _____

14. Are these their thumb tacks? _____

15. Is this Fred's marker? _____

16. Are these Jennifer's pens? _____

17. Are those our papers? _____

18. Those aren't my envelopes. _____

19. These aren't your labels. _____

20. This isn't Andrew's bookcase. _____

Lesson 25 THE VERB *TO BE:* PAST TENSE

Explanation   These are the past tense forms of the verb *to be:*

AFFIRMATIVE	INTERROGATIVE	WITH QUESTION WORDS
I was	was I?	Where was I?
he was	was he?	Where was he?
she was	was she?	Where was she?
it was	was it?	Where was it?
we were	were we?	Where were we?
you were	were you?	Where were you?
they were	were they?	Where were they?

NEGATIVES	CONTRACTIONS
I was not	I wasn't
he was not	he wasn't
she was not	she wasn't
it was not	it wasn't
we were not	we weren't
you were not	you weren't
they were not	they weren't

We use the past tense with these time expressions:

last Monday	five years **ago**	**yesterday**
last June	a while **ago**	**before**
last week	an hour **ago**	
last year	three months **ago**	

Practice A   With a partner, underline the past tense of the verb *to be.* Then answer the TRUE or FALSE questions.

Thanksgiving Day

Last Thursday, it was Thanksgiving Day. Because this is an important holiday in the United States, all the banks and offices were closed. City College in San Diego was closed, too. There weren't any English classes on that day.

Most tourist attractions, stores, and restaurants were open on Thanksgiving Day. Many English students were at work or at home with their families and friends. Some students were out of town for the day. The weather was wonderful. It wasn't too hot, but it wasn't rainy or cool either. It was perfect fall weather. All the parks and beaches were crowded.

Some of the English students were at their teacher's place for Thanksgiving dinner. They were happy to spend the holiday together, and they were curious about this traditional North American holiday.

Write "true" or "false" after each statement.

Thanksgiving Day is on a Thursday.   _____ **true** _____

Thanksgiving Day is in the summer.   _____

Schools are closed on Thanksgiving Day.   _____

Stores are always closed on Thanksgiving Day.   _____

There's a special meal on Thanksgiving Day.   _____

Banks are open on this holiday.   _____

Thanksgiving Day is a holiday all over the world.   _____

Some people go out of town for Thanksgiving.   _____

Practice B   Answer the questions about your last holiday. Then get the same information from your partner.

	ME	MY PARTNER
What was the holiday?	_____	_____
Where were you?	_____	_____
Who were you with?	_____	_____
What was the weather like?	_____	_____
Were you happy or sad?	_____	_____

Report to the class about your partner's last holiday.

Practice C   Walk around. Talk to as many people as possible. Wrtie the information on the chart. Ask these questions:

> Where were you last weekend?
> Who were you with?

	NAME	LOCATION	WITH WHOM
1.			
2.			
3.			
4.			
5.			
6.			
7.			
8.			
9.			
10.			
11.			
12.			
13.			
14.			
15.			

Where were most people last weekend? _____

Practice D   Find people in your class who were at eight of these places recently. Ask these questions:

> Were you at the library recently?
> When were you at the library?

PLACE   NAME   WHEN

at work _____

at a shopping center _____

at a park _____

at a party _____

at night school _____

at the movies _____

at a friend's place _____

at the doctor's office _____

in the gym _____

out of town _____

out of the country _____

List two other places.

1. _____

2. _____

Write about three of your classmates.

1. _____

2. _____

3. _____

Find two people *not* in your class who were at two of these places recently. Report to the class.

NAME   LOCATION   WHEN

1. _____

2. _____

Practice E   Talk to as many people as possible. Ask these questions:

> Where were you two years ago?
> Were you happy or sad?
> Why?

	NAME	LOCATION	HAPPY OR SAD	REASON
1.				
2.				
3.				
4.				
5.				
6.				
7.				
8.				
9.				
10.				
11.				
12.				
13.				
14.				
15.				

Where were most of your classmates two years ago? _____

Practice F   Stand up. Walk around and talk to as many classmates as possible. Ask these questions:

> Where were you born?
> When were you born?

	NAME	PLACE OF BIRTH	YEAR OF BIRTH
1.			
2.			
3.			
4.			
5.			
6.			
7.			
8.			
9.			
10.			
11.			
12.			
13.			
14.			
15.			

On which continent were most of your classmates born?

_____

Explanation   Use *at* for buildings or places when the meaning is general. Use *in* for cities or countries, or to mean *inside* a specific building or place. With a few nouns we don't use prepositions.

at church	in San Diego	go downtown
at school	in Seattle	go home
at home	in New York	go outside
at work	in Poland	go downstairs
at a park	in Japan	
at a party	in Mexico	
at a restaurant	in the library	
at the dentist's		
at the library		
at the movies		

Practice A   Answer these questions. Then find out the same information from a partner.

ME   MY PARTNER

Where were you last night?

_____   _____

Where were you last summer?

_____   _____

Where were you last Saturday night?

_____   _____

Where were you last New Year's Eve?

_____   _____

Where were you two months ago?

_____   _____

Where were you on your last vacation?

_____   _____

Where were you after school yesterday?

_____   _____

Practice A   Work with a partner. Use the past tense of the verb *to be* in these sentences. Check each other's work.

1. They ___were___ at school yesterday.

2. The student ___was___ at the nurse's office an hour ago.

3. Stephanie _____ downtown last night.

4. We _____ at the registration office before lunch.

5. They _____ at a bowling alley several nights ago.

6. _____ you at the shopping center last night?

7. Matthew (negative) _____ at the doctor's office last week.

8. _____ Michael and John at the movies last Saturday?

9. I (negative) _____ in Europe last summer.

10. It _____ very cold here last winter.

11. _____ it hot in Florida last December?

12. The U.S.A. and Canada _____ colonies a long time ago.

13. My neighbors _____ at a party last weekend.

14. David (negative) _____ thin two years ago.

15. _____ you out of town on the long weekend?

16. They (negative) _____ at work yesterday evening.

17. _____ the students outside at lunch time?

18. _____ Sean at the ball game last Sunday?

19. She _____ upstairs a little while ago.

20. Who _____ that at the door a few minutes ago?

21. It (negative) _____ dark at 7:30 last night.

22. _____ the dictionary expensive?

Practice B   Work with a partner. Change the tense of the verbs in these sentences to the past.

1. I'm in a hurry. _____ *I was in a hurry yesterday.* _____

2. They're at the gym. _____ *last night.*

3. Penny is a waitress. _____ *many years ago.*

4. The teacher is in the office. _____ *a while ago.*

5. The janitor's outside. _____ *a few minutes ago.*

6. The men are at the restaurant. _____ *last night.*

7. Their wives are downtown. _____ *yesterday.*

8. The children are polite. _____ *last week.*

9. She's very thin. _____ *before.*

10. They aren't very friendly. _____ *some time ago.*

11. Are you worried about something? _____ *before?*

12. Ron isn't neat. _____ *several years ago.*

13. Is there student parking at the college? _____ *before?*

14. Are you glad to see him? _____ *last week?*

15. There's someone here to see you. _____ *a while ago.*

16. There aren't any stores here. _____ *a long time ago.*

17. We are very nervous. _____ *before the last test.*

18. She isn't quiet and shy. _____ *last night.*

19. Are the buses crowded? _____ *yesterday?*

20. Am I on time? _____ *yesterday evening?*

Practice C   Work with a partner. Change these statements into questions.

1. San Francisco was a small town 100 years ago.

_____*Was San Francisco a small town 100 years ago?*_____

2. There were a lot of wooden houses downtown then.

_____?

3. Houses were inexpensive at that time.

_____?

4. The streets downtown were narrow.

_____?

5. The traffic was very light.

_____?

6. Streetcars were the usual form of transportation.

_____?

7. The downtown area was very small.

_____?

8. The city hall was an old wooden building.

_____?

9. The police station was inside the city hall.

_____?

10. The people were very friendly then.

_____?

11. There were farms close to the city.

_____?

12. Life was very simple 100 years ago.

_____?

Ask five questions about your city 100 years ago.

1. _____

2. _____

3. _____

4. _____

5. _____

Practice D Work with a partner. Write negative statements.

1. Larry was at the party. ____ *Larry wasn't at home last night.* ____

2. They were quite sick. ____ *They weren't healthy last year.* ____

3. We were at the nurse's office. _____

4. Ellen was at a shopping center this morning. _____

5. We were at school yesterday. _____

6. Jennifer was at a park last Saturday. _____

7. She was a bookkeeper many years ago. _____

8. You were at the movies last night. _____

9. He was at work this morning. _____

10. It was closed yesterday. _____

11. The weather was lovely last month. _____

12. I was at my friend's place last night. _____

13. My hair was long two years ago. _____

14. She was shy as a child. _____

15. He was a teller in the bank. _____

Practice E Work with a partner. Look at these notes about Kevin's trip to France last October.

weather .... very nice
traffic .... terrible
pollution .... awful
people .... friendly and polite
food .... delicious
cities .... crowded
streets .... not very clean
wine .... not expensive
hotels .... comfortable, not cheap
public transportation .... fast, modern

```
some parts of Paris ........................ not safe at night
historical old buildings ............................ beautiful
countryside ...................................................... pretty
trip .......................................... wonderful, expensive
```

With your partner describe Kevin's trip.

Kevin was in France last fall.
The weather was very nice.

_____

_____

_____

_____

_____

_____

What was the last big city you were in? _____

What was the weather like? _____

What were the people like? _____

What was the food like? _____

What were the restaurants and hotels like? _____

What were the prices like? _____

Now get the same information from your partner.

_____

_____

_____

_____

Lesson 28 TERMS OF ADDRESS

Explanation In English, the first name usually comes before the surname:

> John Mckay
> Barbara Stevens
> David Bolton

In speaking, in casual conversations, we usually address people by their first names. If we do not know the other person very well, if the situation is formal, or if we want to show extreme respect, we use these titles:

Mr.	....	for men: Mr. John Mckay, or Mr. Mckay
Mrs.	....	for married women: Mrs. Barbara Stevens, or Mrs. Stevens
Miss	....	for single women: Miss Amanda Davis, or Miss Davis
Ms.	....	for both married and single women: Ms. Stevens; Ms. Davis. We use *Ms.* mostly in writing. Not many people say *Ms.* Instead we avoid *Mrs.* and *Miss* by saying the full name without the title: Barbara Stevens; Amanda Davis.
Dr.	....	for doctors, dentists, veterinarians, and others with doctoral degrees: Dr. Jones.
Reverend	....	for religious ministers: Rev. Edwards
Father	....	for Catholic priests: Father Fitzpatrick
Rabbi	....	for Jewish religious leaders: Rabbi Josephson

Formal and Casual Conversation When we talk to people we don't know in formal situations, our conversations are formal. When we talk to close friends or family members, our conversations are casual.

Example:

> Formal conversation
>
> A: Good morning, Mrs. Stevens. I believe you are the bank manager.
> B: Yes. How may I help you?
> A: I'm Dr. McKay. My business partner, Mr. Bolton, and I would like to make an appointment with you to discuss mortgages.

> Casual conversation
>
> A: Hi, Barb. You look great.
> B: Thanks, John. What's new?
> A: Not much, but my buddy Dave and I want the three of us to get together sometime soon and talk about the good old days at school.

Practice A

With a partner, decide three places where formal conversations take place.

1. _____

2. _____

3. _____

What are three places where casual conversations take place?

1. _____

2. _____

3. _____

Practice B

With a partner, decide if these terms of address are formal or casual.

Rev. Carr _____   Mrs. Mitchell _____

Mr. Jack Pritchard _____   Kevin _____

Bobby _____   Kenny _____

Ms. Joanne Jefferson _____   Liz _____

Dick _____   Lisa _____

Miss James _____   Mr. Charles _____

Danny _____   Miss Kelly _____

Dr. Stone _____	Dr. Best _____
Jenny _____	Al _____
Dr. Ann Taylor _____	Mr. Alexander _____
Sue _____	Mr. Edward _____

Lesson 29   EXPRESSIONS OF GREETING

Explanation   There are formal and casual expressions of greeting. Which expression we use depends on how well the speakers know each other and where they are.

Practice A   With a group, categorize the expressions of greeting.

	Formal	Casual
Good morning		
Hello		
Hi		
How's it going?		
What's up?		
Hiya		
Good evening		
Good afternoon		
Just the person I'm looking for!		
Look who's here?		
Whaddaya say?		
Hello, stranger		
Good day		
Speak of the devil!		

Practice B   Choose a partner. Practice greeting each other and responding in formal and casual ways.

Explanation   There are also formal and casual ways of saying good-bye. The expression we use depends on how well the speakers know each other and where they are.

Practice A   With a group, decide if these expressions are formal or casual.

Good-bye _____   Good night _____

'Bye now _____   Well, I'm off _____

So long _____   Don't be a stranger _____

See you _____   Good afternoon _____

Catch you later _____   Have a good day _____

See ya later _____   Talk to you soon _____

Have a good evening _____   Good day _____

Nice talking to you _____   Take care _____

'Bye-bye _____   Have a good one _____

'Bye for now _____

Practice B   Choose a partner. Practice saying good-bye and answering in formal and casual ways.

Day to Day Life

Lesson 1 | SIMPLE PRESENT TENSE

Explanation   We use the **simple present tense** for an action or state that is always true.

Examples:
Richard **comes** from Poland.
He **lives** at 3462 Lakeshore Drive in Chicago.
He **has** a large family.
Richard and his family **have** a nice apartment.
They **like** their neighborhood.

These are the forms of the simple present tense:

AFFIRMATIVE	INTERROGATIVE	WITH QUESTION WORDS
I work	Do I work?	Why do I work?
you work	Do you work?	When do you work?
we work	Do we work?	When do we work?
they work	Do they work?	Why do they work?
he works	Does he work?	Where does he work?
she works	Does she work?	When does she work?
it works	Does it work?	How does it work?

NEGATIVES	CONTRACTIONS
I do not work	I don't work
you do not work	you don't work
we do not work	we don't work
they do not work	they don't work
he does not work	he doesn't work
she does not work	she doesn't work
it does not work	it doesn't work

Pronunciation Note   Pronounce the 3rd person singular ending *s* as *iz* if the verb ends in a sibilant sound:
he pushes   she watches   he fixes.
Pronounce the ending *s* as *z* if the verb ends in a voiced sound:
she lives   he studies   it rewinds.
Pronounce the ending s as s if the verb ends in a voiceless consonant such as *p, t, k, f:*
he stops   she works   he laughs.

Spelling Note   1. If a verb ends in a sibilant sound (*s, z, sh, ch, j*), spell the 3rd person singular ending with *es:* she presses, he wishes, it mixes.
2. If a verb ends in a consonant and *y*, change the *y* to *i* and add *es* for the 3rd person singular: I carry, she carries.

Practice A

With a partner, read the story and circle the **simple present tense.** Then answer the TRUE or FALSE questions.

Two Opinions

My neighbor, Victoria, comes from Sao Paulo, Brazil, but she lives in Buffalo now. She speaks Portuguese and English. She says that she likes Buffalo very much because it has a small town feeling about it. I don't think I agree with her.

I believe Buffalo has a lot of good things. For example, I like the shopping centers and the sports here. We live in a friendly neighborhood. We know a lot of nice people in our community.

However, there are a lot of problems here in Buffalo. The downtown streets don't look safe at night. Some neighborhoods don't have the money to renovate. We need more parks and community centers. The downtown area needs more fancy shops, restaurants, and theaters. The lakefront needs a clean-up too.

Victoria doesn't think Buffalo needs any improvements. She likes it just the way it is. She doesn't want to change anything.

Put "true" or "false" next to each statement.

1. Victoria lives in Sao Paulo, Brazil.

2. The writer lives in Buffalo.

3. Victoria lives in Buffalo.

4. The writer doesn't like Buffalo.

5. Victoria likes Buffalo.

6. Victoria thinks Buffalo needs some changes.

7. The writer wants some changes in the city.

8.. The writer thinks Buffalo needs more parks and theaters.

9. The lakefront is very pretty.

10. The writer doesn't like the downtown area.

Practice B   Work with a partner. Use the information to make statements, as in the examples.

1. Name: Wendy Reid

   Location: San Diego
   Language: English

   a. Wendy Reid lives in San Diego.

   b. She speaks English.

2. Name: Jim and Michelle Belle

   Location: Detroit
   Language: French

   a. Jim and Michelle Belle live in Detroit.

   b. They speak French

3. Name: Ryan Lang

   Location: New York City
   Language: English

   a. _____

   b. _____

4. Name: Daniel Basso

   Location: Mexico City
   Language: Spanish

   a. _____

   b. _____

5. Name: Al and Sarah Small

   Location: Denver
   Language: English

   a. _____

   b. _____

6. Name: Maria and Nick Roth

   Location: Toronto
   Language: German and English

   a. _____

   b. _____

7. Name: Suzanne Lee

   Location: San Francisco
   Language: Chinese

   a. _____

   b. _____

8. Name: Terry and Cathy Fitz

   Location: Chicago
   Language: Greek and English

   a. _____

   b. _____

9. Name: Jules Joffrin

   Location: Montreal
   Language: French

   a. _____

   b. _____

10. Name: Roger and Jane Campo

   Location: Boston
   Language: Italian and English

   a. _____

   b. _____

Find three people not in your class. Report to the class.

1. Name: _____

   Language: _____   a. _____

   Location: _____   b. _____

2. Name: _____

   Language: _____   a. _____

   Location: _____   b. _____

3. Name: _____

   Language: _____   a. _____

   Location: _____   b. _____

Practice C   Walk around and talk to all your classmates. Ask these questions:

> Where do you come from?
> What language do you speak?

	NAME	COUNTRY	LANGUAGE
1.			
2.			
3.			
4.			
5.			
6.			
7.			
8.			
9.			
10.			
11.			
12.			

	NAME	COUNTRY	LANGUAGE
13.			
14.			
15.			

How many different languages do your classmates speak? _____

Write about two of your classmates.

1. _____

_____

2. _____

_____

Outside Class

Talk to two people not in your class. Find out the same information.

1. _____

_____

2. _____

_____

Lesson 2	**THE VERB *TO HAVE:* HOUSING**

Explanation These are the forms of *to have* in the **simple present tense.**

AFFIRMATIVE	INTERROGATIVE	WITH QUESTION WORDS
I have	Do I have?	What do I have?
you have	Do you have?	What do you have?
we have	Do we have?	What do we have?
they have	Do they have?	What do they have?
he <u>has</u>	<u>Does</u> he have?	What do<u>es</u> he have?
she <u>has</u>	<u>Does</u> she have?	What do<u>es</u> she have?
it <u>has</u>	<u>Does</u> it have?	What do<u>es</u> it have?

NEGATIVES	CONTRACTIONS
I do not have	I don't have
you do not have	you don't have
we do not have	we don't have
they do not have	they don't have
he do<u>es</u> not have	he doe<u>s</u>n't have
she do<u>es</u> not have	she do<u>es</u>n't have
it do<u>es</u> not have	it do<u>es</u>n't have

Examples: They **have** a nice apartment.
Melissa **has** a large bedroom.
Do they **have** a garage?
Does the apartment **have** a lot of windows?
What kind of place **do** you **have**?
Why **does** she **have** a roommate?
We **don't have** a dish washer.
He **doesn't have** a washing machine.

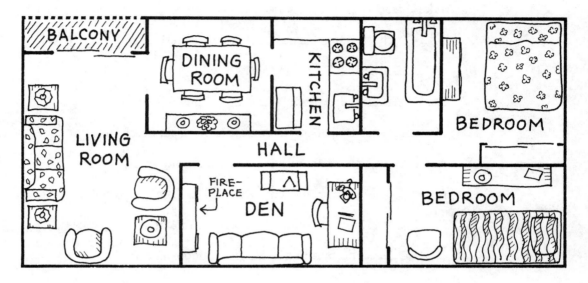

Practice A   With a partner, read the story and circle the verb *to have*. Then use the correct form of *to have* in the sentences.

The Apartment

Wendy Reid lives with a roommate, Emily McKay. Their apartment is very large. It has two bedrooms, a living room, a kitchen, a separate dining room, and a den. There is a balcony off the living room and a fireplace in the den. There is a skylight in the dining room.

In the apartment building, there is a laundry room, a fitness center, and a swimming pool, but no elevator. This is a problem for Wendy and Emily because they live on the top floor of the building. The building isn't new but it is in good condition and it has rent control. The landlord allows pets but not children. Wendy has a cat, and Emily has a canary.

1. Wendy Reid __*has*__ a two-bedroom apartment.

2. Wendy and her roommate _____ a big place.

3. Wendy and Emily _____ a balcony.

4. The dining room _____ a skylight.

5. The living room _____ a fireplace.

6. The building _____ an elevator.

7. They _____ a brand new apartment.

8. They _____ a swimming pool.

9. The building _____ a fitness center.

10. Wendy and Emily _____ children.

11. They _____ pets.

12. The apartment building _____ a laundry room.

Make questions. Use the verb *to have*.

1. _Does_ the kitchen _have_ a dishwasher?

2. _____ they _____ pay T.V.?

3. _____ the bedrooms _____ big closets?

4. _____ the bathroom _____ a separate shower?

5. _____ the balcony _____ a sliding door?

6. _____ Wendy and Emily _____ nice neighbors?

7. _____ all the rooms _____ carpets?

8. _____ the building _____ indoor parking?

9. _____ the kitchen _____ a lot of cupboards?

10. _____ they _____ an indoor pool?

11. _____ the building _____ a doorman?

12. _____ Wendy and Emily _____ new appliances?

13. _____ the building _____ a security guard?

14. _____ the apartment _____ a fire extinguisher?

15. _____ Wendy and Emily _____ any problems?

fire
extinguisher   fitness center   porch   fireplace

What does your place have?

Practice B   Housing Questionnaire: Circle the correct answers for you.

1. I live: alone   with my family   with a roommate   other

2. I live in: an apartment   a flat   a room   a house

3. My place has: 1 bedroom   2 bedrooms   3 bedrooms   other

4. My place has: a balcony   a yard   a skylight   a fireplace

5. My place has: a living room   a dining room   a den   a fire extinguisher

6. My place has: a garage   a doorman   a security system   a porch

7. I have: a swimming pool   a sauna   a fitness center   low rent

8. I have: pets   children   nice neighbors   a landlord

Practice C   Write four things about your place.
Write four things about your partner's place.

Practice D   With your partner read this advertisement and write TRUE or FALSE after each statement.

For Rent in a Shared House

[18 Garnet Ave., near College and University]
A large sunny room
   available July 1st
   $358 per month + utilities
A smaller room
   available Aug. 1st
   $300 per month + utilities
Lots of Living Space
   —front yard and porch
   —living room, dining room, den, rec room, laundry
   —backyard
   —large kitchen with fireplace
   —3 bathrooms
   —basement with plenty of storage space
Quiet Neighborhood
   —call **488-9925** [Pat, Lynda]

---

1. The large room costs $300 per month.   **false**

2. The large room is sunny. _____

3. The living room has a fireplace. _____

4. The total cost of the small room is $300 per month. _____

5. The rooms are in an apartment building. _____

6. The rec room has a lot of storage space. _____

7. The large room costs more than $358 per month. _____

8. The tenant has the use of the backyard and front yard. _____

9. Pat and Lynda have more information about the rooms. _____

10. There is a lot of storage space in the basement. _____

Practice E   Walk around and talk to as many classmates as possible. Fill in the chart. Ask these questions:

> What kind of place do you have?
> How many bedrooms do you have?
> How many bathrooms do you have?
> What special features does your place have?

NAME	KIND OF ACCOMMO-DATION	NUMBER OF ROOMS	NUMBER OF BATHROOMS	SPECIAL FEATURES
1.				
2.				
3.				
4.				
5.				
6.				
7.				
8.				
9.				
10.				
11.				

NAME	KIND OF ACCOMMO-DATION	NUMBER OF ROOMS	NUMBER OF BATHROOMS	SPECIAL FEATURES
12.				
13.				
14.				
15.				

What kind of accommodation do most people have?

_____

Lesson 3 **FOODS**

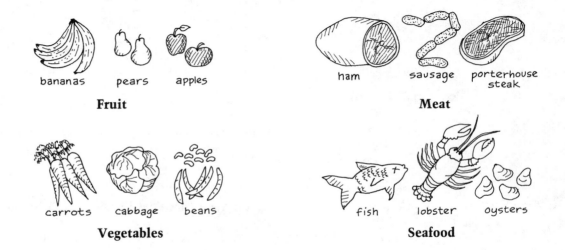

bananas pears apples		ham sausage porterhouse steak
Fruit		**Meat**
carrots cabbage beans		fish lobster oysters
Vegetables		**Seafood**

Practice A   Work with a group. Arrange the foods in the correct categories.

chicken	fish	apples	oranges
carrots	eggs	cabbage	pizza
pasta	lettuce	rice	potato chips
beef	lobster	tomatoes	potatoes
shrimp	broccoli	bananas	plums
pears	grapes	turkey	pork
ham	oysters	lamb	sausage
soup	stew	yogurt	ice cream
cheese	veal	chocolate	hamburgers
cauliflower	cake	hot dogs	beans

	FRUIT	VEGETABLES	MEAT	SEAFOOD	OTHER

Practice B Answer the questions. Then get the same information from your partner.

	ME	MY PARTNER
What is your favorite meat?	_____	_____
What is your favorite seafood?	_____	_____
What is your favorite dessert?	_____	_____
What is your favorite fruit?	_____	_____
What is your favorite vegetable?	_____	_____
What is your favorite snack?	_____	_____

Practice C Work with a partner. Circle the food that doesn't belong in each group.

1. ham   sausage   veal   chicken   chocolate

2. apples   cabbages   oranges   grapefruit   pears

3. carrots   plums   bananas   pineapple   peaches

4. turkey   beef   oysters   duck   hot dogs   sausage

5. cake   lobster   fish   shrimp   clams   mussels

6 cheese   pie   milk   ice cream   butter

7. potatoes   cauliflower   onions   beans   yogurt

8. lamb   veal   ham   pizza   pork   hamburgers

Lesson 4	SIMPLE PRESENT TENSE: NEGATIVE

Explanation   The negative forms are:

I
you }don't . . .
we
they

he
she }doesn't . . .
it

Examples: I don't like spaghetti.
David doesn't like chicken.
We don't like salads.
She doesn't like Chinese food.

Practice A   Talk to as many classmates as possible. Ask these questions:

> What food do you like a lot?
> What food don't you like?

	NAME	LIKES	DISLIKES
1.			
2.			
3.			
4.			
5.			
6.			
7.			
8.			
9.			
10.			
11.			
12.			
13.			
14.			
15.			

Practice B   With a partner, read this and then write "TRUE" or "FALSE after each statement."

GOLDFINGER'S PUB

PATIO

NOW   OPEN

MON. – SAT. 11:30–2:00 A.M.

SUN. 12:00 Noon – Midnight

GREAT NIGHTLY SPECIALS

MON: STEAK NIGHT. . . . $6.99

TUES: CHICKEN WINGS. . . . $4.99

WED: PIZZA w/CAESAR SALAD . . . $4.99

THURS: BURGER NIGHT. . . . $3.99

FRI: FISH & CHIPS . . . $4.99

**PLUS TRADITIONAL PUB FARE
12 GREAT BEERS ON TAP !!**

39 COLLEGE STREET

---

1. The pub is open until 2:00 A.M. every night.   _____ **false** _____

2. The special on Thursday is hamburgers.   _____

3. People can only order the daily specials.   _____

4. There are twelve different kinds of beer at this pub.   _____

5. The pub is open for breakfast.   _____

6. The special on Tuesday is chicken.   _____

7. On Wednesday the salad is included in the price of the pizza.   _____

8. The restaurant serves a lot of steaks on Monday.   _____

9. The name of the restaurant is Goldfinger's Pub.   _____

10. Friday's special is french fries and fish.   _____

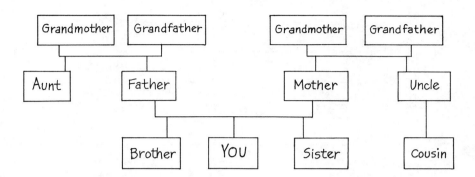

Explanation   These are the words we use in English for family relationships:

parents	children	sister	niece
mother	daughter	brother	cousin
father	son	aunt	wife
grandmother	granddaughter	uncle	husband
grandfather	grandson	nephew	in-laws

Practice A   Draw a picture of your family tree. Include your grandparents, your parents, your brothers and sisters, your uncles and aunts, and your cousins.

How many people are there in your immediate family? _____

Who is your next of kin? _____

Write about your relatives. Then write about your partner's relatives.

MY FAMILY   MY PARTNER'S FAMILY

My family lives _____   _____

I have _____   _____

_____   _____

_____   _____

_____   _____

Who is your favorite relative? _____

Who is your partner's favorite relative? _____

Practice B   Talk to all the people in your class. Ask these questions:

How many brothers and sisters do you have?
Where do they live?

	NAME	BROTHERS	SISTERS	COUNTRY
1.				
2.				
3.				
4.				
5.				
6.				
7.				
8.				
9.				
10.				
11.				
12.				
13.				
14.				
15.				

Who is an only child? _____

Who comes from the biggest family? _____

Lesson 6 THE VERB PHRASE *HAVE GOT*

Explanation   *Have got* has the same meaning as the verb *to have.* These are the forms of *have got:*

AFFIRMATIVE	CONTRACTIONS	EXAMPLES
I have got	I've got	I've got a problem.
you have got	you've got	You've got a cold.
we have got	we've got	We've got some money.
they have got	they've got	They've got some work.
he <u>has</u> got	he'<u>s</u> got	He'<u>s</u> got the book.
she <u>has</u> got	she'<u>s</u> got	She'<u>s</u> got a sandwich.
it <u>has</u> got	it'<u>s</u> got	It'<u>s</u> got a bone.

NEGATIVE	CONTRACTIONS	EXAMPLES
I have not got	I haven't got	I haven't got a problem.
you have not got	you haven't got	You haven't got a cold.
we have not got	we haven't got	We haven't got any money.
they have not got	they haven't got	They haven't got any work.
he has not got	he hasn't got	He hasn't got the book.
she has not got	she hasn't got	She hasn't got a sandwich.
it has not got	it hasn't got	It hasn't got a bone.

INTERROGATIVE	EXAMPLES
have I got?	Have I got a problem?
have you got?	Have you got a cold?
have we got?	Have we got any money?
have they got?	Have they got any work?
has he got?	Has he got the book?
has she got?	Has she got a sandwich?
has it got?	Has it got a bone?

Practice A   Work with a partner. Use *have got* to replace *have* in the sentences.

1. Rachel has thirty cousins. _____ *Rachel's got thirty cousins* _____.

2. Do you have any brothers? _____

3. How many sisters do you have? _____

4. Does Megan have any uncles? _____

5. Joshua has three brothers. _____

6. How many nieces does Amanda have? _____

7. I don't have any nephews. _____

8. We don't have any children. _____

9. Justin has some relatives in the U.S.A. _____

10. Nicole doesn't have a big family. _____

11. You have the wrong number. _____

12. Do you have any change? _____

13. Does James have a lot of time? _____

14. They don't have a car. _____

15. My friend doesn't have a lot of money. _____

16. Do you have any questions? _____

17. Sarah doesn't have the address of the store. _____

18. Does she have the phone number? _____

Practice B   What's something new or special you've got? Circle it below.

a new apartment   a new book

new furniture   a new T.V. set

new dishes   a stereo

a new compact disk   clothes

OTHER _____   _____

_____   _____

Talk to as many people as possible. Ask them:

> What's something new you've got?
> Why do you like it?

	NAME	OBJECT	REASON
1.			
2.			
3.			
4.			
5.			
6.			
7.			
8.			
9.			
10.			

Practice A   Work with a partner. Label the parts of the body in the picture. Check your spelling with the list of parts of the body.

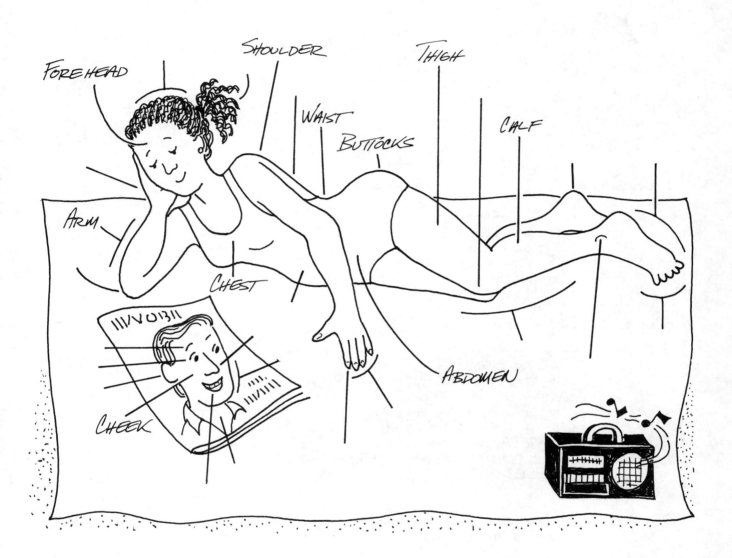

Parts of the Body

head	chin	forehead	eye
mouth	eyebrow	eyelash	nose
cheek	ear	neck	shoulder
back	chest	stomach	waist
buttocks	thigh	leg	hair
knee	calf	ankle	heel
fingers	toes	fingernail	lips
elbow	abdomen	foot	teeth
wrist	hand	arm	face

Explanation   These are some expressions to describe physical problems:

Headache   **Stomachache**   **The flu**

I don't feel well.   I've got a cough.
I've got a cold.   I've got a fever.
I've got a headache.   I've got a backache.
I've got a stomachache.   I've got a sore throat.
I've got the flu.

Practice A   Practice this conversation with your partner:

> A: I feel terrible.
> B: What's the matter with you?
> A: I think I've got a cold.
> B: Have you got a sore throat, too?
> A: No, I haven't, but I really feel awful.
> B: Well, why don't you go to bed, and call
>   the doctor if you don't feel better soon?

Now choose another physical problem. Replace the underlined words. Make up a conversation with your partner.

Practice B

Explanation   We describe physical problems in this way:

I have a pain in my stomach.	**or**	I've got a stomachache.
I have a pain in my back.	**or**	I've got a backache.
I have a pain in my head.	**or**	I've got a headache.
I have a pain in my ear.	**or**	I've got an earache.
I have a pain in my tooth.	**or**	I've got a toothache.
I have a pain in my neck.	**or**	I've got a sore neck.
I have a pain in my leg.	**or**	I've got a sore leg.
I have a pain in my arm.	**or**	I've got a sore arm.

In a less formal way we say:

My stomach hurts.
My leg hurts.
My tooth hurts.

With a partner, make statements using *ache* or *sore*.

1. Her stomach hurts. _____ *She's got a stomachache.* _____

2. Daniel's arm hurts. _____ *Daniel's got a sore arm.* _____

3. Jessica's back hurts. _____

4. John's legs hurt. _____

5. Your throat hurts. _____

6. His ear hurts. _____

7. Laura's tooth hurts. _____

8. My head hurts. _____

9. Andrew's arms hurt. _____

10. Her neck hurts. _____

11. Marie's elbow hurts. _____

12. Brian's ankle hurts. _____

13. Their wrists hurt. _____

14. Our knees hurt. _____

15. Eric's and Adam's shoulders hurt. _____

16. My hands hurt. _____

17. Their eyes hurt. _____

Lesson 9 SHORT ANSWERS

Explanation   These are some short answers to questions:

QUESTION	SHORT ANSWERS		
Do you work?	Yes, I do.	or	No, I don't.
Are you a student?	Yes, I am.	or	No, I'm not.
Were you late?	Yes, I was.	or	No, I wasn't.
Do you have a brother?	Yes, I do.	or	No, I don't.
Have you got some money?	Yes, I have.	or	No, I haven't.

Practice A   Ask questions to find people in the class who fit these descriptions. Please remember to use the correct question form and short answers.
Find someone in the class who:

NAME

drives to school. _____

has got a pet. _____

lives alone. _____

is an only child. _____

has an apartment. _____

was at the movies last weekend. _____

doesn't have a car. _____

doesn't smoke. _____

likes to do homework. _____

has got a big family. _____

speaks more than two languages. _____

lives in a high-rise building. _____

is happy today. _____

doesn't sleep in on Sundays. _____

likes school. _____

doesn't like summer. _____

has got a headache. _____

doesn't pay rent. _____

Lesson 10   SIMPLE PRESENT TENSE: HABITUAL ACTIONS

Explanation   We use the **simple present tense** for habitual or repeated actions.

Examples:
I **get** up early on weekdays.
I **take** the bus to work every day.
I **start** work at half past eight.
My roommate **doesn't get** up early.
She **doesn't take** the bus to work.
She **drives** to work.
We **get** home late in the afternoon.
We **don't go** out in the evening very often.
We usually **watch** T.V. and then we **go** to bed.

These are some of the adverbs and adverb phrases we use with the simple present tense:

every day	in the afternoon	at night
on weekdays	in the morning	once a week
on Mondays	in the evening	twice a year

Practice A   With a partner, read the story and circle the **simple present tense.** Then use the correct form of the verb in the sentences.

City Life

Atlanta has a population of over two million people. It is a busy city in the southeastern United States. On weekdays most people get up between 6 A.M. and 8 A.M. Many people drive to work every day. Others take public transportation. The morning rush hour is between 7 A.M. and 9 A.M., when every one hurries to work.

Most employees arrive at work at about 9 o'clock. They work until noon. They usually have one hour off for lunch. After that they work until 5 or 6 P.M. Most businesses close at this time. Then the afternoon rush hour begins as all these people hurry to get home.

In the evenings Atlanta is an exciting and lively city. Many people go out in the evenings. They go out to dinner, to the movies, or to sports events. Some people prefer to stay home and relax. They have supper, and then they watch television or get together with friends.

1. Michael (be) ___*is*___ from Atlanta.

2. He (live) _____ downtown but he (work) _____ in an office in the suburbs.

3. He (get) _____ up at 7 o'clock in the morning.

4. He (leave) _____ his apartment at 8 o'clock.

5. He (drive) _____ to work.

6. He (get) _____ to work at 8:45 A.M.

7. The people in his office (have) _____ a coffee break at around 10:30 in the morning.

8. They (eat) _____ lunch at 12:30.

9. The employees (finish) _____ work at 5 P.M.

10. Michael (arrive) _____ home at 5:45 in the afternoon.

11. He (read) _____ the newspaper and (relax) _____.

12. Michael and his friends (go) _____ out for dinner twice a week.

13. Most of the time, he (stay) _____ home and (watch) _____ T.V.

14. Sometimes he (buy) _____ tickets for the theater and (invite) _____ a friend to go with him.

Answer these questions about your routine. Then find out the same information from your partner.

	ME	MY PARTNER
What time do you get up?	_____	_____
When do you go to bed?	_____	_____
What do you do every day?	_____	_____
How often do you eat out?	_____	_____
When do you get together with friends?	_____	_____

Practice B Walk around and ask all the people in the class about their routines on weekdays. Ask these questions:

> What do you do in the mornings?
> What do you do in the afternoons?
> What do you do in the evenings?

NAME	MORNING	AFTERNOON	EVENING
1. _____			
2. _____			
3. _____			
4. _____			
5. _____			
6. _____			

NAME	MORNING	AFTERNOON	EVENING
7.			
8.			
9.			
10.			
11.			
12.			
13.			
14.			
15.			

Write about three classmates:

1. _____

2. _____

3. _____

Practice C   Talk to as many people as possible. Ask these questions:

> How do you get to school?
> How long does it take you?

NAME	HOW	TIME
1.		
2.		
3.		
4.		
5.		
6.		
7.		
8.		
9.		
10.		

	NAME	HOW	TIME
11. _____			
12. _____			
13. _____			
14. _____			
15. _____			

Practice D   With a partner, match the adjectives with the verbs to answer the question, "What do you do when . . .?"

WHAT DO YOU DO WHEN YOU ARE:

happy	cry
sad	smile
thirsty	eat
hungry	rest
tired	apologize
late	go to the doctor
sick	call up a friend
lonely	drink
sorry	hurry

Use the correct form of the verb *to be* and finish the sentences.

1. When Michael __is__ tired, _he rests._____

2. When the children _____ thirsty, _____

3. When Jennifer _____ happy, _____

4. When Marie _____ sad, _____

5. When we _____ hungry, _____

6. When they _____ sick, _____

7. When I _____ late, _____

8. When you _____ lonely, _____

9. When David _____ sorry, _____

10. When my hands _____ dirty, _____

11. When I _____ cold, _____

12. When I _____ warm, _____

Practice E   Answer these questions.

What do you do when you are angry? _____

What do you do when you are lonely? _____

What do you do when you are bored? _____

What do you do when you are homesick? _____

Talk to your classmates. Find out the same information from them.

NAME	ANGRY	LONELY	BORED	HOMESICK
1.				
2.				
3.				
4.				
5.				
6.				
7.				
8.				
9.				
10.				
11.				
12.				
13.				
14.				
15.				

Report the most interesting answer to the class.

_____

Practice F   With a partner, use the correct form of the **simple present tense.**

Marie's Life

Marie (live) _____ in Montreal, Canada.

She (study) _____ English at Concordia University in that city.

Marie (have) _____ a part-time job.

She (work) _____ in a record store on the weekends.

She (meet) _____ a lot of people at work.

Her friends (like) _____ her very much.

She (not have) _____ a lot of money, but she (be) _____ happy in Montreal.

Her relatives (live) _____ in a small town near Quebec City.

They (speak) _____ French but they (not speak) _____ English.

Write about yourself.

1. I (live) _____ in _____ .

2. I (study) _____ at _____ .

3. I (have) _____ a _____ job.

4. I (work) _____ in a _____ .

5. I (meet) _____ .

6. My relatives (live) _____ in _____ .

7. They (speak) _____ .

Now get the same information from your partner.

QUESTIONS	MY PARTNER
1. _Where do you live?_	_____
2. _____	_____
3. _____	_____
4. _____	_____
5. _____	_____
6. _____	_____
7. _____	_____

Practice G   Talk to as many people as possible. Ask them these questions:

> What do you do on Saturdays?
> What do you do on Sundays?

	NAME	SATURDAYS	SUNDAYS
1.			
2.			
3.			
4.			
5.			
6.			
7.			
8.			
9.			
10.			
11.			
12.			
13.			
14.			
15.			

What do most people do on Saturdays? _____

What do most people do on Sundays? _____

Practice H. Job Descriptions

With a partner, match the job descriptions with the occupations.

nurses	builds houses
a plumber	writes newspaper articles
electricians	fixes faucets
hairdressers	plans and cooks meals
waitresses	looks after patients' teeth
salesclerks	repair automobiles
a journalist	answers the telephone
a chef	looks after children
mechanics	make withdrawals and deposits
a dentist	builds brick buildings
a receptionist	keeps a record of accounts
a day-care worker	cleans people's teeth
tellers	wait on tables
a mail carrier	sell in a store
a bricklayer	cut and style hair
a bookkeeper	delivers the mail
a dental hygienist	install electricity
a carpenter	look after patients in hospitals

Write about five occupations.

1. _____

2. _____

3. _____

4. _____

5. _____

Speak to three people *not* in your class. Ask them:

> **What's your job?**
> **What do you do?**

1. _____

2. _____

3. _____

Practice I. More Job Descriptions

In English we form the names of some occupations by adding *er* to the verb.

Examples:

> Sharon **teaches** French. She is a French teacher.
> They **play** the guitar. They are guitar players.

With a partner, tell what these people do in their jobs every day.

1. Michael is an office manager. _____*He manages an office for a living.*_____

2. Linda is a ballet dancer. _____*She dances in a ballet company.*_____

3. Wendy Reid is an English teacher. _____

4. Emily McKay is a bus driver. _____

5. Victoria Charles is a singer. _____

6. Ryan Lang is a guitar player. _____

7. Stephanie and I are writers. _____

8. Sarah and Al are factory workers. _____

9. Jim Belle is a house painter. _____

10. Fred and Sharon are computer operators. _____

11. Suzanne Lee is a baker. _____

12. Michelle is a bank manager. _____

13. Thomas is a construction worker. _____

14. Robert is a window washer. _____

15. Eric and Steven are waiters. _____

16. Rachel and I are dressmakers. _____

17. Jordan is a T.V. news reporter. _____

18. Christopher is an office cleaner. _____

19. Ellen and James are clothing designers. _____

20. Matthew is a printer. _____

Write about two people in your class

1. _____

2. _____

Write about two people *not* in your class.

1. _____

2. _____

Report to the class.

Lesson 11 | ADVERBS OF FREQUENCY

Explanation

ADVERB	MEANING
always	100% of the time
usually	about 80–90% of the time
often	about 70% of the time
sometimes	about 50% of the time
rarely	about 5% of the time
never	0% of the time

Position of Adverbs:

with the verb *to be*   I am **always** on time.
                        We're **never** late.
with other verbs   I **always** get to work on time.
                        We **never** arrive late.

Practice A   Work with a partner. Use adverbs in these sentences.

1. (always)   They take the bus. _____ *They always take the bus.* _____

2. (never)   She is happy. _____ *She is never happy.* _____

3. (often)   They go out to the movies. _____

4. (usually)   He is tired after work. _____

5. (sometimes)   We take a taxi when we're late. _____

6. (usually)   Students are nervous about tests. _____

7. (rarely)   Teachers make mistakes. _____

8. (often)   We do our homework in the library. _____

9. (never)   She works on weeknights. _____

10. (always)   He sings when he's happy. _____

11. (sometimes)   We were lonely. _____

12. (often)   Was he sad? _____

13. (usually)   We were relaxed on our holiday. _____

14. (sometimes)   Was she late for work? _____

15. (rarely)   Cats are friendly. _____

16. (always)   He isn't busy. _____

17. (sometimes)   We are angry. _____

18. (often)   They don't speak to their neighbors. _____

19. (never)   Does he apologize? _____

20. (always)   Do they eat sandwiches when they're hungry? _____

21. (usually)   Do they drink beer when they're thirsty? _____

22. (rarely)   They are sick. _____

Practice B   Work with a partner. Use the correct form of the verb and the adverb in these sentences.

1. Sharon (always, be) ___is always___ on time for her English class.

2. She (never, take) _____ a taxi to school.

3. She (usually, get) _____ up very early.

4. Her classmate, Kevin, (often, be) _____ late for school.

5. He (sometimes, get) _____ a ride to school from his roommate.

6. The traffic (usually, be) _____ very heavy during rush hour.

7. Kevin and Sharon (never, miss) _____ their English classes.

8. The classes (never, be) _____ boring.

9. The teacher (always, bring) _____ interesting things to talk about.

10. The students (always, learn) _____ something new.

11. The class (sometimes, go) _____ out on field trips.

12. They (usually, visit) _____ a tourist attraction or a special place.

13. The field trips (rarely, be) _____ to out-of-town locations.

14. The students (often, have) _____ interesting questions.

15. They (always, write) _____ a report or a story about the trip.

Write three things your class *always* does.

1. _____

2. _____

3. _____

Write three things your class *never* does.

1. _____

2. _____

3. _____

Practice C   Talk to the people in your class about their routines. Put their answers on the chart. Ask these questions:

> What do you always do on Saturdays?
> What do you never do on weeknights?
> What do you often do on weekends?
> What do you sometimes do after school?

	NAME	ALWAYS	NEVER	OFTEN	SOMETIMES
1.					
2.					
3.					
4.					
5.					
6.					
7.					
8.					
9.					
10.					
11.					
12.					
13.					
14.					
15.					

Explanation The interrogative forms are:

TO BE PRESENT	*TO BE* PAST	SIMPLE PRESENT
am I?	was I?	do I . . .?
is he?	was he?	does he . . .?
is she?	was she?	does she . . .?
is it?	was it?	does it . . .?
are we?	were we?	do we . . .?
are you?	were you?	do you . . .?
are they?	were they?	do they . . .?

Practice A. Questions in a Department Store

Excuse me, where do you sell cosmetics?

On the first floor, next to the ladies' sports wear.

With a partner, rewrite these questions used in a department store. Use the correct interrogative form, and please use a conversation opener.

Conversation openers:

> Pardon me
> Excuse me
> I'm sorry to bother you, but . . .

1. (be) _Pardon me. Are_ the escalators near the main entrance?

2. (sell) _Excuse me._ Where _do_ you _sell_ cosmetics?

3. (be) _____ Where _____ the fitting rooms?

4. (cost) _____ How much _____ this sweater _____?

5. (be) _____ _____ the sales tax included?

6. (come) _____ _____ this sweater _____ in a larger size?

7. (give) _____ _____ you _____ special discounts to students?

8. (be) _____ _____ the men's suits on this floor?

9. (be) _____ _____ winter boots on sale last week?

10. (carry) _____ _____ you _____ these belts in smaller sizes?

11. (have) _____ _____ you _____ this purse in different colors?

12. (be) _____ what _____ the total price before tax?

13. (exchange) _____ where _____ I _____ this shirt?

14. (have) _____ where _____ you _____ men's underwear?

15. (sell) _____ _____ this store _____ greeting cards?

16. (accept) _____ _____ you _____ personal checks?

17. (take) _____ which credit cards _____ you _____ ?

18. (be) _____ where _____ the cash register?

19. (be) _____ how much _____ this blouse?

20. (be) _____ how much _____ it before the sale?

21. (return) _____ where _____ we _____ these slippers?

22. (be) _____ _____ these skirts on sale yesterday?

Now think of four other questions to ask in a department store.

1. _____

2. _____

3. _____

4. _____

Practice B With a partner, change these statements to the interrogative.

1. The magazines are on the table. _____*Are the magazines on the table?*_____

2. The bookstore accepts credit cards. _____ ?

3. The groceries were on the counter. _____ ?

4. There are a lot of mistakes in his work. _____ ?

5. There was a sale at the department store. _____ ?

6. The doctor writes prescriptions. _____ ?

7. Electricians make a lot of money. _____ ?

8. The women were friendly and kind. _____ ?

9. Jessica eats a lot of junk food. _____ ?

10. These chocolates are very expensive. _____ ?

11. Robert drives very fast. _____ ?

12. The patients need medical insurance. _____ ?

13. There's a drinking fountain nearby. _____ ?

14. Her relatives speak French. _____ ?

15. Ellen gets up very early. _____ ?

16. Michael goes out twice a week. _____ ?

17. We've got the tickets. _____ ?

18. Her husband has a new job. _____ ?

19. They are healthy. _____ ?

20. The radio is on. _____ ?

21. Tony speaks Greek. _____ ?

22. Megan's got a stomachache. _____ ?

23. The English test was easy. _____ ?

24. The coffee machine was out of order. _____ ?

25. Laura likes cauliflower. _____ ?

Lesson 13   REVIEW OF NEGATIVES

Explanation

The negative forms are:

TO BE PRESENT	TO BE PAST	SIMPLE PRESENT TENSE
I'm not	I wasn't	I don't . . .
he isn't	he wasn't	he doesn't . . .
she isn't	she wasn't	she doesn't . . .
it isn't	it wasn't	it doesn't . . .
we aren't	we weren't	we don't . . .
you aren't	you weren't	you don't . . .
they aren't	they weren't	they don't . . .

Practice A. Apartment Living Downtown

With a partner, use negatives in these sentences.

1. (be)   There _____*aren't*_____ very many inexpensive apartments downtown.

2. (have)   Most new buildings _____ rent control.

3. (live)   Laura _____ in a new high-rise building.

4. (be)   The apartments in Laura's building _____ expensive.

5. (make)   Most of the tenants in the building _____ a lot of money.

6. (ask)   The landlord _____ for references.

7. (have)   The tenants _____ leases.

8. (have got)   The building _____ a swimming pool or a fitness center.

9. (provide)   The landlord _____ free parking.

10. (be)   Laura's bachelor apartment _____ very modern.

11. (work)   The refrigerator _____ very well most of the time.

12. (be)   The windows _____ very large.

13. (have got)   The apartment _____ new carpets or fresh paint.

14. (be)   The elevator _____ very fast.

15. (be)   The machines in the laundry room _____ in good condition.

16. (know)   Most of the neighbors _____ each other.

17. (be)   The carpets in the halls _____ very clean.

18. (be)   The area _____ dangerous twenty years ago.

19. (be)   The neighborhood _____ poor then.

20. (be)   There _____ a lot of stores in the area then.

21. (be)   Neighbors _____ unfriendly at that time.

Practice B   Work with a partner. Change these sentences to the negative.

1. The weather was warm. _____ *The weather wasn't warm.* _____

2. He sells expensive clothes. _____ *He doesn't sell expensive clothes.* _____

3. Birds make good pets. _____

4. My roommate is shy. _____

5. They share the expenses. _____

6. I like cereal. _____

7. I take the bus to work on Mondays. _____

8. The secretaries were very friendly and helpful. _____

9. The carpenter fixes filing cabinets. _____

10. My friend's got a car. _____

11. The dishes were on the counter. _____

12. Nurses work long hours. _____

13. He drives downtown every day. _____

14. Victoria is a very popular lady. _____

15. They were at the hospital a month ago. _____

16. My cousin was lonely. _____

17. Ellen speaks Spanish well. _____

18. Sarah and Andrew are good singers. _____

19. A dental hygienist makes a lot of money. _____

20. Plumbers need special tools. _____

21. Her parents go out twice a week. _____

22. I need your help. _____

Lesson 14 SUBJECT AND OBJECT PRONOUNS

Explanation   We use **pronouns** in place of names. But we use different **pronouns** for different places in the sentence.

Examples: 1. **Eric** likes **Adam.**   2. **Wendy** lives with **Emily.**
                   He likes **him.**   **She** lives with **her.**
                SUBJECT   OBJECT   SUBJECT   OBJECT

SUBJECT PRONOUNS	OBJECT PRONOUNS
I	me
he	him
she	her
we	us
they	them
you	you
it	it

Practice A   With a partner, underline the names and then change the names to **pronouns**.

1. Kevin likes Sarah. _____ *He likes her.* _____

2. Rachel knows Ryan. _____

3. Adam and Laura like the Rolling Stones. _____

4. Amanda and I work with Eric. _____

5. Stephanie likes Danielle. _____

6. Jennifer knows David and me. _____

7. Emily likes Michael J. Fox and Michael Jackson. _____

8. Jordan talks to Ashley and Nicole every day. _____

9. Michelle and I like "Anne of Green Gables." _____

10. Justin writes to Megan. _____

11. Ryan and Joshua like you and Steven. _____

12. Matthew helps Joseph and me. _____

13. Daniel knows Robert and John. _____

14. Melissa thinks about her aunt. _____

15. Thomas and James worry about their uncle. _____

Lesson 15 PRESENT CONTINUOUS TENSE: ACTIONS IN PROGRESS

Explanation   The **present continuous tense** shows that an action is in progress at the moment of speaking. To form the present continuous tense, use the verb *to be* and add *ing* to the verb stem.

AFFIRMATIVE	INTERROGATIVE	WITH QUESTION WORDS
I am working	Am I working?	Why am I working?
he is working	Is he working?	Why is he working?
she is working	Is she working?	Why is she working?
it is working	Is it working?	How is it working?
we are working	Are we working?	Why are we working?
you are working	Are you working?	Where are you working?
they are working	Are they working?	Why are they working?

CONTRACTIONS

I'm working
he's working
she's working
it's working
we're working
you're working
they're working

NEGATIVES

I am not working
he is not working
she is not working
it is not working
we are not working
you are not working
they are not working

CONTRACTIONS

I'm not working
he isn't working
she isn't working
it isn't working
we aren't working
you aren't working
they aren't working

Examples: I**'m looking** at my book.
The students **are thinking** about verbs now.
We**'re reading** the explanation.
The teacher **is explaining** at this moment.

We use these time expressions with the present continuous tense:

now
at this moment
this very minute
at the present time

Practice A   With a partner, look at these actions. Circle the actions of the people in your class.

eating	drinking	writing
working	reading	sitting
standing	listening	looking
thinking	talking	whispering
drawing	smiling	whistling
sleeping	scratching	walking
cleaning	chewing	studying

Write three things you are doing right now.

1. _____

2. _____

3. _____

Write about your partner.

1. _____

2. _____

3. _____

Write about three other students in the class.

1. _____

2. _____

3. _____

Write about someone *not* in your class.

_____

_____

Practice B   Work with a partner. What are people doing in these places now?

At the grocery store
The customers _____

The cashier _____

At the bank
The tellers _____

The clients _____

At the hospital

A nurse _____

The patients _____

At the train station

The passengers _____

The ticket agent _____

At the library

Some students _____

The librarian _____

At the dentist's office

The dentist _____

The receptionist _____

Practice C Talk to as many classmates as possible. Ask them:

> What's your best friend's name?
> Where is your best friend now?
> What do you think he or she is doing right now?

	NAME	FRIEND'S NAME	LOCATION	ACTIVITY
1.				
2.				
3.				
4.				
5.				
6.				
7.				
8.				
9.				
10.				
11.				
12.				
13.				
14.				
15.				

Practice D   Here are the names of some famous people. With your partner, write what you think they are doing at this time.

1. Mick Jagger   (famous singer)

   He's making a new record now. _____

2. The Rolling Stones   (singers)

   _____

3. Wayne Gretzky   (hockey player)

   _____

4. Michael Jackson   (singer and dancer)

   _____

5. Sylvester Stallone and Robert DeNiro   (actors)

   _____

6. Jane Fonda   (fitness expert)

   _____

7. Ben Johnson   (Olympic sprinter)

   _____

8. Madonna   (singer and movie star)

   _____

9. Paul McCartney   (song writer)

   _____

10. Diego Maradona   (soccer player)

   _____

Think of two other famous people. What do you think they are doing now?

1. _____

2. _____

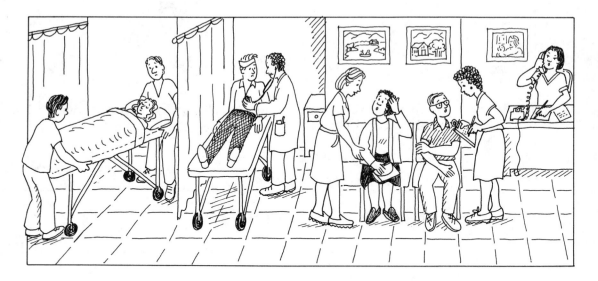

Practice E. The Emergency Department

With a partner, rewrite these sentences with the **present continuous tense.** Use time expressions such as *now, at this moment, at this time.*

1. The emergency department at City Hospital gets busy on weekends.

   The emergency department at City Hospital is getting busy now.
   _____

2. The receptionist answers the telephone.

   _____

3. The ambulance attendants bring in new patients.

   _____

4. Does the secretary fill out medical forms?

   _____

5. The nurses look after the patients.

   _____

6. The laboratory technicians take blood samples.

   _____

7. The X-ray technician takes X-rays.

   _____

8. The hospital pharmacy sends medicine to the emergency department.

_____

9. The nurses don't examine the patients.

_____

10. Does the doctor treat a lot of patients?

_____

11. Do the nurses take the patients' blood pressure?

_____

12. The receptionist doesn't wear a uniform.

_____

13. The hospital volunteers don't work in the emergency department.

_____

14. Do the doctors prescribe medicine?

_____

15. Do the patients wait to see the doctor?

_____

Lesson 16 PRESENT CONTINUOUS TENSE: CONTINUING ACTIONS

Explanation   We use the **present continuous tense** for an activity that is continuing over the present time.

Examples: I**'m taking** a computer course.
Marie**'s trying** to find a full-time job.
David**'s looking** for a new apartment.
They**'re waiting** for their families to come here.

Practice A   What is something important that you are doing at this time?

_____

_____

Walk around and ask your classmates these questions:

> What are you doing at this time?
> How is it going for you?

	NAME	ACTIVITY	SUCCESS
1.			
2.			
3.			
4.			
5.			
6.			
7.			
8.			
9.			
10.			
11.			
12.			
13.			
14.			
15.			

What are many of your classmates doing now? _____

Practice B   Imagine it is 20 years from now. All your dreams have come true.

What year is it? _____

What is your job? _____

Where are you living? _____

What are you doing? _____

Talk to as many classmates as possible. Get the same information from them.

	NAME	POSITION	LOCATION	ACTIVITY
1.				
2.				
3.				
4.				
5.				

	NAME	POSITION	LOCATION	ACTIVITY
6.				
7.				
8.				
9.				
10.				
11.				
12.				
13.				
14.				
15.				

Report the most interesting answers to the class.

Lesson 17   PRESENT CONTINUOUS TENSE: NEGATIVES

Examples:

Wendy Reid smokes, but she **isn't smoking** now because she's working.
She drinks wine, but she **isn't drinking** now because she's teaching.
The students speak other languages, but they **aren't speaking** other languages now because they're practicing English.

Practice A   What are five things you sometimes do but you aren't doing at this moment? Get the same information from your partner.

Me:

1. I _____ but I'm not _____ now because _____

2. I _____ but I'm not _____ now because _____

3. I _____ but I'm not _____ now because _____

4. I _____ but I'm not _____ now because _____

5. I _____ but I'm not _____ now because _____

My partner:

1. _____

2. _____

3. _____

4. _____

5. _____

Practice B
Tense Review

Work with a partner. Use the correct form of the **simple present tense** or the **present continuous tense.**

1. The Neptune Furniture Company (sell) _sells_ office furniture.

2. The company (have) _____ a lot of employees.

3. The company (grow) _____ quickly at this time.

4. Neptune Furniture (look) _____ for more employees now.

5. The employees (not, work) _____ on the weekend.

6. The company (pay) _____ its employees every two weeks.

7. The employees (get) _____ good salaries.

8. The employees (not belong) _____ to a union.

9. All the employees (be) _____ very friendly and polite.

10. The Neptune Furniture Company (have) _____ a large office.

11. Some people (work) _____ in the office at this moment.

12. The secretary (mail) _____ bills now.

13. The receptionist (make) _____ appointments every day.

14. The office clerks (not, file) _____ at this moment.

15. (speak) _____ the bookkeepers _____ to the accountant now?

16. There (be) _____ a large warehouse next to the office.

17. The office manager (meet) _____ with the foreman every morning.

18. The foreman (give) _____ instructions to the workers daily.

19. The inspector (not check) _____ the furniture now.

20. (send) _____ the shipper _____ out some chairs today?

21. The workers (not take) _____ a coffee break right now.

22. How many shifts (be) _____ there?

23. (fill) _____ the workers _____ out a timesheet for each shift?

24. What time (start) _____ the evening shift _____?

25. When (finish) _____ the day shift _____?

Lesson 18 | TALKING ABOUT THE WEATHER

Explanation   These are some ways to describe the weather:

It's cloudy.
It's windy.

It's sunny.

It's foggy.   **It's raining.**

Practice A   With a partner, look at the list. What's the weather like today? Please circle.

It's windy.   It's hailing.
It's foggy.   It's snowing.
It's raining.   The sun is shining.
It's hot.   It's humid.
It's cold.   It's cool.
It's cloudy.   It's overcast.
It's clear.   There's a thunderstorm.
There's a blizzard.   There's a snowstorm.
It's icy.

What's the temperature today? _____

Practice B   Temperatures can be in centigrade or fahrenheit. In the list below the temperature is in centigrade degrees. Read about the temperature in these world cities:

LEGEND: s-sunny pc-partly cloudy c-cloudy sh-showers t-thunderstorms r-rain
sf-snow flurries sn-snow i-ice

CITY	TODAY	TOMORROW
Acapulco	32/22 s	32/22 s
Amsterdam	12/6 c	12/8 c
Athens	14/7 sh	16/9 t
Atlanta	8/4 s	10/−1 s
Baltimore	6/−4 s	4/−3 s
Barbados	28/22 sh	29/22 sh
Beijing	9/−1 pc	9/−2 pc
Berlin	7/2 s	9/4 c
Bermuda	24/21 pc	23/20 sh
Boston	6/−1 pc	4/−2 s
Buenos Aires	27/14 pc	28/14 pc
Cairo	23/11 pc	25/13 pc
Chicago	−2/−9 pc	3/−2 pc
Dallas	15/3 s	17/6 s
Denver	12/−3 pc	9/−7 pc
Frankfurt	9/3 pc	12/6 pc
Geneva	6/1 pc	8/0 pc
Hamburg	9/4 pc	10/4 pc
Honolulu	31/23 pc	29/23 pc
Hong Kong	27/20 sh	26/20 pc

CITY	TODAY	TOMORROW
Houston	16/7 s	18/7 s
Jerusalem	22/10 s	25/10 s
London	11/5 c	13/7 c
Los Angeles	27/12 s	27/12 s
Madrid	13/2 s	11/8 pc
Mexico City	20/2 pc	22/4 pc
Miami	22/14 pc	23/16 s
Montreal	1/–3 sf	2/–3 sf
Moscow	4/–5 pc	–2/–6 sn
New York	6/–1 pc	4/1 s
Paris	13/6 pc	14/7 c
Philadelphia	6/–1 c	3/–2s
Rio de Janeiro	28/21 pc	29/21 pc
Rome	13/9 r	14/7 s
Seoul	13/2 s	12/2 s
St. Louis	1/–4 s	6/0 pc
Tokyo	16/11 s	14/10 s
Toronto	6/2 pc	7/4 s
Vienna	4/–1 r	7/0 c
Warsaw	6/0 pc	8/2 c
Washington	7/2 s	4/0 s

What's the weather like in:

Atlanta _____

Amsterdam _____

Baltimore _____

Denver _____

Cairo _____

Houston _____

Hamburg _____

Montreal _____

Miami _____

Moscow _____

New York _____

Paris _____

Rome _____

Practice C   With a partner, pick a city in the world. Imagine you are visiting the city. Write a postcard to your classmates.

Example:

> Dear Classmates!
> Here we are in Acapulco. The weather is wonderful. The sun is shining. We are sitting on the beach and we're drinking fantastic piña coladas. Wish you were here.
>   Love,
>   Irene and Ellen

Postcard from _____

_____

_____

_____

_____

Practice D Walk around and talk to as many classmates as possible. Ask these questions:

> What country do you come from?
> How many seasons are there in your country?
> What's it like there right now?

NAME	COUNTRY	SEASONS	WEATHER NOW
1.			
2.			
3.			
4.			
5.			
6.			
7.			
8.			
9.			
10.			
11.			
12.			
13.			
14.			
15.			

Compare the weather in one other country to the weather here.

_____

Practice E. Talking About the Weather

When people in North America want to start a conversation they sometimes begin by talking about the weather.

With a partner, look at these conversations about the weather. Decide which ones are positive and which ones are negative.

    A: Wonderful weather we're having.
    B: Yes. It's perfect spring weather.

_____

    A: What awful weather!
    B: It sure is. It's snowing and blowing today.

_____

    A: Hot enough for you?
    B: Are you kidding? I'm boiling, and the humidity is killing me.

_____

    A: Don't you just love this spring weather?
    B: There's nothing like it.

_____

Make one positive comment about today's weather in order to start a conversation.

_____

Make one negative comment about today's weather in order to start a conversation.

_____

Practice talking about the weather to start a conversation. Then act out your conversation for the class.

Practice A. The Cafeteria

With a partner, use *do, does, is, are,* or *am* in the blanks to make correct questions.

1. _____ you eat in the cafeteria every day?

2. _____ your class have lunch at noon?

3. _____ the students ordering hamburgers?

4. _____ the cook bringing more soup?

5. _____ Michael buy chocolate milk?

6. _____ the cashier give change for the pop machine?

7. _____ the students lining up for coffee?

8. _____ Laura drink diet Pop?

9. _____ the janitors clean off the tables?

10. _____ Sarah and Marie paying for their food now?

11. _____ the teachers buy lunch in the cafeteria?

12. _____ Robert eating pizza?

13. _____ they make Italian food here?

14. _____ the English students eat junk food?

15. _____ I taking the last cookie?

16. _____ Rebecca and Emily putting food on their trays?

17. _____ they carrying trays?

18. _____ they serve beer in the cafeteria?

19. _____ the students play cards in the cafeteria?

20. _____ the cafeteria workers put the trays away?

Practice B. Transportation in the City

With a partner, change the statements into questions.

1. The Main Street bus runs every ten minutes.

   Does the Main Street bus run every ten minutes?

2. Passengers need transfers to change buses.

_____

3. Passengers need the exact fare to get on the bus.

_____

4. The seats at the front of the bus are for old or sick people.

_____

5. The passengers are waiting for the next bus.

_____

6. There are special lanes for buses on some streets.

_____

7. The express buses stop at the subway.

_____

8. The subway trains are crowded at rush hour.

_____

9. Rush hour usually begins at 4 P.M.

_____

10. Transit maps are available at the subway stations.

_____

11. There was a problem on the subway yesterday.

_____

12. Many people were late for work.

_____

13. Traffic in this city is increasing.

_____

14. The cost of parking is going up.

_____

15. There was a lot of traffic downtown yesterday morning.

_____

16. Pollution is causing damage.

_____

17. More people are taking public transportation.

_____

18. They are leaving their cars at home.

_____

19. Some people buy special monthly passes.

_____

20. A pass costs less.

_____

21. There are special discounts for students and seniors.

_____

Lesson 20   QUESTION WORDS

Explanation   Here are some question words and their meanings:

Who–person   *Which*–one of two or three
What–thing   *How many*–quantity
Where–place   *How much*–quantity
Whose–possession   *What kind of*–description
When–time   *How*–in what way
Why–reason   *How far*–distance

Practice A   With a partner, use the correct question word in the sentences.

QUESTION   ANSWER

1. __*When*__ do you have lunch?   At half past twelve.

2. __*What*__ are they eating?   Sandwiches.

3. _____ do you take your break?   At half past ten.

4. _____ are they standing in line?   Because it's busy.

5. _____ coffee are you paying for?   Her coffee.

6. _____ are they drinking coffee?   In the cafeteria.

7. _____ do you drink coffee?   In the morning

QUESTION	ANSWER
8. _____ cups do you drink?	Two.
9. _____ is that?	It's my teacher.
10. _____ long is the break?	Fifteen minutes.
11. _____ do you buy for lunch?	Soup and salad.
12. _____ is he carrying so much food?	Because he's hungry.
13. _____ likes hot dogs?	Marie and Linda do.
14. _____ are the soft drinks?	In the cooler.
15. _____ do they serve lunch?	Between 11:30 and 1:00.
16. _____ tray is that?	It's Daniel's.
17. _____ soup are you tasting?	Ellen's.
18. _____ does the cafeteria close?	At seven P.M.

Practice B   With a partner, use the correct question word.

QUESTION	ANSWER
1. __*Who*__ leaves the lights on all day?	Jessica does.
2. __*Where*__ does he park?	In the driveway.
3. _____ music do you like?	Classical music.
4. _____ are you doing?	Relaxing.
5. _____ is the matter with you?	I've got a headache.
6. _____ dictionaries have you got?	Three or four.
7. _____ is he asking for money?	Because he needs some.
8. _____ many sisters do you have?	Two.
9. _____ is your favorite color?	Blue.
10. _____ of car do you want to buy?	An American car.
11. _____ dictionary are you using?	My friend's.
12. _____ of the two books do you prefer?	The new one.
13. _____ are you going home?	At five o'clock.
14. _____ is the registration office?	On the third floor.
15. _____ does it cost to take an English course?	It's free.

16. _____ does Michelle work?   In a government office.

17. _____ is she crying?   Because she's sad.

18. _____ do you like this school?   It's great.

19. _____ do you say that in English?   You say, "You're welcome."

20. _____ is your age?   I'm nineteen.

21. _____ old are you?   I'm nineteen years old.

22. _____ were you born?   In Germany.

23. _____ money do you make?   Not too much.

24. _____ does the train leave for Chicago?   At 6:45 P.M.

25. _____ is it to New York?   It's about 500 miles.

26. _____ of the three tests are we having today?   The first one.

27. _____ of food do you like?   Chinese food.

28. _____ does she do after school?   She babysits.

29. _____ is this class over?   At 9:30.

Starting Out

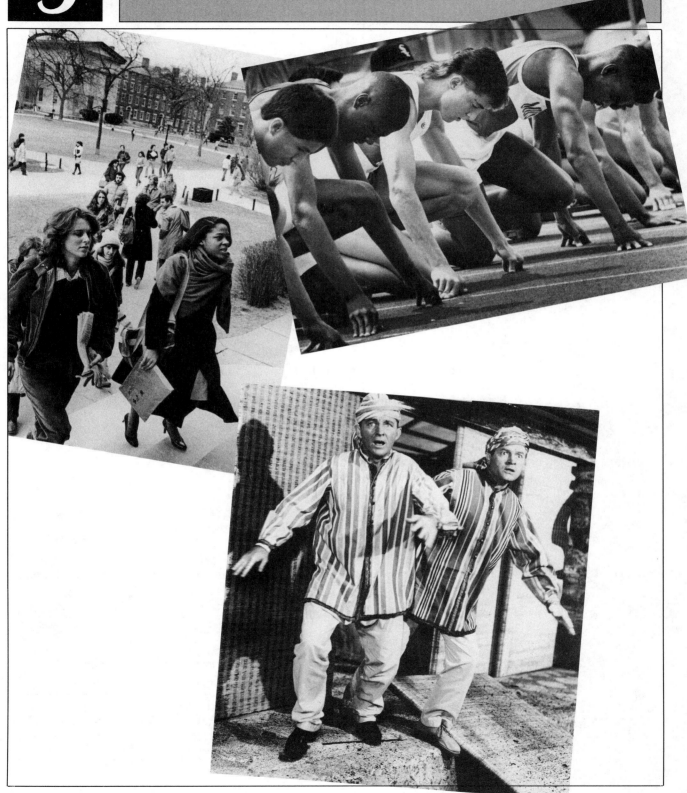

Explanation There are formal and casual ways of introducing yourself.

Examples:

Formal
A: Good morning. I'm Mrs. Jenkins.
B: How do you do? I'm Adam Smith.
A: How do you do?

A: Good evening. I am Reverend Lee.
B: I am Mrs. Adams.
A: Pleased to meet you.

Casual
A: Hi, there! The name's Ted. What's yours?
B: Samantha, but everybody calls me Sam.
A: Nice to meet you, Sam.

A: Hi, I'm Jess.
B: I'm Danny
A: Glad to meet you, Danny.

Practice A With a partner, decide three places where formal and casual introductions take place.

FORMAL   CASUAL

_____   _____

_____   _____

_____   _____

Take turns introducing yourself to your partner in formal and casual ways. The teacher will ask you to act out your introductions for the class. Decide where your introductions are taking place.

FORMAL   CASUAL

_____   _____

INTRODUCING OTHERS

Explanation　When we introduce someone else, the introduction can be formal or casual. This depends on where the introduction is taking place and on the situation. When we introduce another person, we usually add some information about that person so that a conversation can begin.

Examples:

Formal
A. I'd like to introduce Jessica Jenkins. She's from Canada.
B. It's a pleasure to meet you.

Casual
A. This is Jess. She's an architect.
B. Hi, Jess. Good to meet you.

Practice A　Work with a partner. Get the information on the chart from your partner. Then team up with another pair and introduce your partner. Continue until you have introduced three partners.

	PARTNER #1	PARTNER #2	PARTNER #3
First Name			
Surname			
Nickname			
Nationality			
Hobby			
Profession			
Pet Peeve			

Lesson 3 **STARTING A CONVERSATION**

Explanation　In every language there are ways to show that people like each other and want to start a conversation. In English, one way of starting a conversation with a classmate or a peer is to compliment.

Example:

Wendy:　Charlie, I really like your yellow sweater.

Charlie:　Thanks, Wendy. It's brand new. It was a birthday gift from my girlfriend.

COMPLIMENTS	RESPONSES
I like . . .	Thank you. It's new.
I love . . .	Thank you. It was a gift.
Your . . . is fantastic.	Thanks. It's from France.
Your . . . is wonderful.	Thanks, but it's old.
That . . . looks great on you.	Thanks. Do you really like it?
That . . . looks terrific.	Thanks. Your . . . looks great, too. Is it new?

Practice A With a partner, think of some things to compliment people about.

_____   _____

_____   _____

Practice complimenting and responding.

COMPLIMENTS	RESPONSES
_____	_____
_____	_____
_____	_____

With your partner, act out a conversation for the class. Outside the class, speak to one person. Compliment him or her. Tell the class about it.

Lesson 4 COUNT/MASS NOUNS

Explanation English nouns can be countable or uncountable.

COUNTABLE NOUNS

have a plural form (cup, cups)
we use *many* with countable nouns
we use *a few* with countable nouns

UNCOUNTABLE NOUNS

don't have a plural form (tea)
we use *much* with uncountable nouns
we use *a little* with uncountable nouns

Examples:

	COUNTABLE	UNCOUNTABLE
Singular	An apple is a good snack.	Coffee is a strong drink.
Plural	Apples are good for you.	
much/many	How many apples are there?	How much coffee is there?
a lot of	There are a lot of apples.	There's a lot of coffee.
a little/a few	There are a few apples.	There's a little coffee in the pot.
some	Let's buy some apples.	Let's buy some coffee.
any	Don't buy any apples.	Don't buy any coffee.

These nouns are usually uncountable:

	Examples
liquids	coffee, tea, perfume, oil, paint
small, granular things	sugar, salt, sand, dust, rice
materials	gold, cotton, wood, glass, steel
gases	air, hydrogen, pollution
some categories of food	meat, bread, fish, fruit, cheese

Some other uncountable nouns are: *money, time, weather, hair, furniture,* and abstract nouns such as *love, health, happiness.*

PLEASE NOTE: Most uncountable nouns can become countable if we change the meaning of the noun to include *kinds of* or *varieties of.*

Examples:

The perfumes of France are famous.
Indian cottons are inexpensive.
The cheeses are in the next aisle.

Practice A   Work with a partner. Circle the things there are in your fridge, and underline those in your partner's fridge.

apples	cream	oranges	juice	cheese
chicken	butter	fish	milk	soda pop
beans	ham	jam	hot dogs	bananas
eggs	ice cream	onions	bread	ketchup
carrots	tomatoes	lettuce	peanut butter	beef
potatoes	sliced meat	beer	wine	honey
vegetables	cake	soup	mustard	shrimp

Tell what's in your fridge and in your partner's fridge.

MY FRIDGE   MY PARTNER'S FRIDGE

There _____   There _____

_____   _____

_____   _____

_____   _____

_____   _____

Practice B   With a partner, make questions. Use *much* or *many*.

1. There's some coffee in the pot. _____*How much coffee is there?*_____.

2. There are some glasses in the sink. _____*How many glasses are there?*_____.

3. There's some salt in the box. _____

4. There are some napkins in the drawer. _____

5. There were some cookies on the counter. _____

6. There was some rice in the bowl. _____

7. There's some oil in the bottle. _____

8. There were some tea bags in the box. _____

9. There's some vinegar in the bottle. _____

10. There were some carrots on the counter. _____

11. There are some sandwiches in the fridge. _____

12. There's some whiskey in the bottle. _____

Practice C   Work with a partner. Use *much* or *many* in the blanks.

1. I don't have ___*much*___ money.

2. Please don't eat so ___*many*___ chocolates.

3. Don't make so _____ noise.

4. Is there _____ butter on the toast?

5. I don't have _____ friends here.

6. We don't know _____ people in this city.

7. He doesn't like _____ salt and pepper on his food.

8. Hurry! We don't have _____ time.

9. Do you want _____ sugar in your coffee?

10. There weren't _____ students in the cafeteria.

11. Were there _____ textbooks in the bookstores?

12. Please don't drink so _____ wine.

13. Is there _____ snow on the streets?

14. We aren't buying _____ fruit.

15. Are you making _____ sandwiches?

Practice D   Work with a partner. Use *a little* or *a few* in the blanks.

1. I take ____*a little*____ sugar in my coffee.

2. There were ____*a few*____ cigarettes in the package.

3. They speak _____ English.

4. There are _____ mistakes in your work.

5. I have _____ problems with my English.

6. There's _____ flour in the bag.

7. David's buying _____ flowers.

8. There are _____ dishes in the sink.

9. They need _____ help with their homework.

10. There's _____ water on the floor.

11. Thomas drinks _____ milk when he's thirsty.

12. She takes _____ aspirins when she has a headache.

13. There were _____ people in the library last night.

14. She's got _____ boyfriends.

15. Kevin takes _____ syrup when he's got a cough.

Explanation   *Some* means an unspecified number or amount.

Examples: I have **some** money.
There are **some** eggs in the refrigerator.

In questions, we use *some* if we think the answer is positive. We use *any* if we think the answer is negative.

Examples: Do you have **some** money? (I think so)
Do you have **any** money? (I don't think so)

In negatives, we **must** use *any*.

Examples: I don't have **any** money.
There aren't **any** eggs in the refrigerator.

Practice A. Grocery Shopping

With a partner, use *some* or *any* in these sentences.

1. There are _____*some*_____ specials at the supermarket today.

2. Do we need _____ groceries?

3. We don't have _____ fruit.

4. We haven't got _____ vegetables.

5. There aren't _____ eggs left.

6. Is there _____ fresh bread?

7. Isn't there _____ meat left in the freezer?

8. We haven't got _____ toilet paper or detergent.

9. We need to do _____ shopping.

10. There are _____ shopping carts at the front of the store.

11. There are _____ vegetables on sale today.

12. They haven't got _____ fresh lettuce.

13. They don't have _____ fish on special.

14. Have they got _____ cheese on sale?

15. Are you buying _____ meat?

16. Let's get _____ coffee and soft drinks.

17. Are you buying _____ more groceries?

18. Let's go. I don't have _____ money left.

Explanation   We use expressions of measure such as *a bottle of . . . a slice of . . .* with uncountable nouns. This permits us to count them. We can also use these with countable nouns.

Examples: Uncountable nouns:
five slices of bread
two bottles of wine
three yards of cotton
two ounces of gold

Countable nouns:
a dozen oranges
a can of beans
a box of cookies

a can   a bottle   a slice   a jar   a box

an ear of corn   a tube   a dozen eggs   a head of lettuce

Practice A   Work with a partner. Match the expressions of measure to the nouns.

a can of	cigarettes
a bar of	gum
a tube of	jam
a box of	chocolates
a carton of	soup
a jar of	soda pop
a bottle of	cake
a dozen	wine
a slice of	butter
a case of	grapes
a package of	bread
a piece of	corn
a pound of	eggs
a kilogram of	toothpaste
a head of	soap
an ear of	lettuce
a bunch of	ham
a loaf of	beef

Practice B   With a partner, answer these requests. Use the right expressions of measure.

1. I need some soap. _____*There's a bar of soap in the bathroom cabinet.*_____

2. I'd like some gum. _____*There's a package of gum on the kitchen table.*_____

3. I need some toothpaste. _____

4. I'd like some pop. _____

5. We need some eggs. _____

6. I'd like a glass of wine. _____

7. We'd like some bread. _____

8. They need some butter. _____

9. He'd like some strawberry jam. _____

10. She'd like some lettuce. _____

11. We'd like some ham. _____

12. She'd like some corn. _____

13. He'd like a cigarette. _____

14. We'd like some soup. _____

15. They'd like some grapes. _____

Lesson 7 | ORDER OF ADJECTIVES

Explanation   We put adjectives before nouns in English.

Examples: The **big** car is in the parking lot.
There was a **little** dog outside.

When there is more than one adjective, we put the adjectives in this order:

DETERMINER	OPINION	SIZE	AGE	COLOR	ORIGIN	MATERIAL	NOUN
the	beautiful	big	new	white	Italian	leather	sofa
my	expensive	little		black	French	silk	scarf

Most of the time we do not use so many adjectives. We usually use only two or three adjectives together.

Examples: I'm buying **some black wool** gloves.
He drives **a sporty new Italian** car.

Practice A   Work with a partner. In each of the examples below, put all the ideas together to make one sentence.

1. He drives a sports car. It is red. It is new.

   He drives a new red sports car.

2. She is reading a novel. It is short. It is English.

   _____

3. Charles wears pullovers. They're wool. They're expensive.

   _____

4. I'm using a pen. It's cheap. It's black. It's plastic.

   _____

5. Are you carrying your briefcase? It's new. It's leather.

   _____

6. She looks great in her coat. It's fur. It's stylish.

   _____

7. Where do you buy those shirts? They're silk. They're long.

   _____

8. We live in a house. It's brick. It's big. It's old.

   _____

9. That's a lovely rug. It's old. It's Persian.

   _____

10. I'd like some coffee. I want it black. I want it strong.

    _____

11. He's got a belt. It's snake-skin. It's elegant. It's brown.

    _____

12. Would you like some red wine? It's Spanish. It's delicious.

    _____

13. They like cookies. They're chocolate-chip. They're large.

    _____

14. He's got a beard. It's black. It's long.

_____

15. I've got a knife. It's red and white. It's small. It's new.

_____

16. Show me your key case. It's green. It's expensive. It's new.

_____

Practice B   Describe these things, and then get the same information from your partner.

	ME	MY PARTNER

your favorite
  piece of clothing: _____   _____

  piece of jewelry: _____   _____

  piece of furniture: _____   _____

  store: _____   _____

  restaurant: _____   _____

Practice C   With a partner, write a commercial for a restaurant, a store, or a product such as a food or a drink.

Examples: Do you like good Italian food?
Do you like romantic Italian music?
Do you like an elegant small dining room?
If you do, come to Portofino, our city's best Italian restaurant.

Your commercial:

_____

_____

_____

_____

_____

Report to the class. Decide which commercial you like the best.

Practice D   With a partner, put these words into correct English sentences.

1. glass / wood / like / a / German / cold / beer / you / of / ?
        Would you like a glass of cold German beer?
_____

2. perfume / French / she / 's / a / bottle / expensive / buying / of

_____

3. skirt / wearing / is / Linda / long / silk / yellow / a

_____

4. drinking / Spanish / sweet / wine / red / of / pitcher / are / we / a

_____

5. red / like / new / leather / your / really / I / jacket

_____

6. got / jar / expensive / of / mustard / a / imported / French / have / we / ?

_____

7. cake / would / like / a / delicious / you / chocolate / piece / of / ?

_____

8. need / loaf / Italian / a / fresh / we / of / white / bread / do / ?

_____

9. bowl / of / eating / he / a / soup / thick / delicious / pea / 's

_____

10. beautiful / gold / your / watch / new / is / ?

_____

11. love / your / white / new / leather / I / sofa / Italian

_____

12. pair / he / wants / of / shoes / patent / a / black / his / birthday / for / leather

_____

13. on / dress / long / great / wool / red / that / looks / you

_____

14. painting / she / got / 's / French / small / an / interesting

_____

15. those / cost / how / leather / soft / Italian / gloves / much / do / ?

_____

16. buying / gold / expensive / 's / an / she / bracelet

_____

17. wearing / comfortable / cotton / shirt / red / is / he / a

_____

18. he / buy / to / wooden / desk / large / 'd / like / a / old

_____

19. borrow / new / English / to / dictionary / brand / I / 'd / like / your

_____

Lesson 8 | ADJECTIVES: COMPARATIVES

Explanation

When we compare two people or things, we use the comparative degree. Short adjectives (one syllable) add *er* to the adjective. We use *than* in the comparison.

Examples: Sarah is taller than Emily.
Sarah is older than Emily.

Adjectives of two syllables ending in *y* also add *er* to form the comparative.

Examples: Sarah is prettier than Emily.
Sarah is friendlier than Emily.

Spelling Note

Two-syllable adjectives ending in *y* change the *y* to *i*

Example: I'm angrier than George is.

Most adjectives follow these rules, but there are a few two-syllable adjectives which do not end in *y* and which also add *er* to form the comparative degree.

Examples: narrow—narrower than
handsome—handsomer than
gentle—gentler than

Practice A

Compare yourself to your classmates. Talk to as many people as possible to complete the chart. Here are some questions to ask:

> How tall are you?
> How much do you weigh?
> How old are you?
> How strong are you?
> Are you busy?
> Do you get good grades?

	NAME	COMPARISON
Example:	Sam _____	**is** friendl**ier than I am.**
	_____	tall _____
	_____	short _____
	_____	heavy _____
	_____	light _____
	_____	old _____
	_____	young _____
	_____	big _____
	_____	small _____
	_____	thin _____
	_____	busy _____
	_____	quiet _____
	_____	strong _____
	_____	weak _____
	_____	smart _____

Practice B Work with a partner. Make comparisons of the different students in your class. Decide which adjectives you want to use.

ADJECTIVES:

_____   _____

_____   _____

COMPARISONS:

_____

_____

_____

_____

_____

Practice C   With a partner, read this and answer the TRUE or FALSE questions.

FACT SHEET ON THE WORLD'S HIGHEST STRUCTURES

STRUCTURE	HEIGHT	LOCATION	DATE COMPLETED
Eiffel Tower	1052 ft. 4 in. (320.7 meters)	Paris	1889
Empire State Building	1250 ft. (381 meters)	New York City	1931
World Trade Center	1350 ft. (411.4 meters)	New York City	1973
Sears Tower	1454 ft. (443 meters)	Chicago	1974
The C.N. Tower	1822 ft. 1 in. (555.3 meters)	Toronto	1975

1. The Eiffel Tower is in Paris.   **true**

2. The Empire State Building is higher than the Eiffel Tower.   _____

3. The Sears Tower is in New York City.   _____

4. The Sears Tower is higher than the World Trade Center in New York. _____

5. The C.N. Tower is lower than the Sears Tower.   _____

6. The C.N. Tower is older than the Sears Tower.   _____

7. The World Trade Center is newer than the C.N. Tower.   _____

8. The Empire State Building is older than the Eiffel Tower.   _____

9. The C.N. Tower is in Chicago.   _____

10. The Sears Tower is older than the World Trade Center in New York. _____

Practice D   Compare the following things. Use the adjectives in the list.

COMPARE

an apple / a chocolate bar
a record / a compact disk
a bicycle / a car
the subway / the bus
beer / whiskey
an airplane / a ship
planes / trains
the city / the country
a big city / a small town
summer vacation / Christmas vacation
hamburgers / vegetables
an elephant / a lion
a tiger / a monkey
cats / dogs
roses / daisies
men / women
reading / writing
houses / apartments
the Sears Tower / the Empire State Building

ADJECTIVES

healthy
cheap
safe
fast
strong
large
slow
dirty
busy
long
healthy
large
brave
friendly
pretty
strong
easy
big
high

1. _____ *An apple is healthier than a chocolate bar.* _____

2. _____

3. _____

4. _____

5. _____

6. _____

7. _____

8. _____

9. _____

10. _____

11. _____

12. _____

13. _____

14. _____

15. _____

16. _____

17. _____

18. _____

19. _____

Practice E   Work with a partner. Make a comparative statement about each of these topics.

Animals   Example: Horses are bigger than donkeys.

_____

_____

Children   Example: A child is happier than an adult.

_____

_____

Countries   Example: Korea is smaller than Canada.

_____

_____

Transportation   Example: The Concorde is faster than a DC 10.

_____

_____

Weather   Example: Summer is warmer than spring.

_____

_____

Practice F

Explanation   When we want to show that two things or two people are the same in some way, we use this structure *as . . . as.*

Examples: I am **as** tall **as** you are.
Ted is **as** tall **as** Linda is.

It's also possible to use the negative.

Examples: I'm **not as** short **as** Marie.
Linda isn**'t as** tall **as** Ted.

With a partner, make comparative statements with the same meaning as these sentences.

1. City air isn't as clean as country air.

   Country air is cleaner than city air.

2. The city isn't as quiet as the country.

   _____

3. Life in the city isn't as healthy as life in the country.

   _____

4. Life in the country isn't as busy as life in the city.

   _____

5. Prices in the city aren't as low as prices in the country.

   _____

6. People in the city aren't as friendly as people in the country.

   _____

7. The city isn't as safe as the country.

   _____

8. Roads in the country aren't as busy as roads in the city.

   _____

9. People in the country aren't as rich as people in the city.

   _____

10. People in the city aren't as happy as people in the country.

    _____

11. The food in the city isn't as fresh as food in the country.

    _____

12. Life in the city isn't as slow as life in the country.

    _____

13. Life in the city isn't as good as life in the country.

    _____

Write your own comparisons of life in the city and life in the country.

_____

_____

_____

| Lesson 9 | ADJECTIVES: SUPERLATIVES |

Explanation   When we compare more than two people or things, we use the **superlative degree.** Adjectives of one syllable add *est* to form the superlative. We use *the* with the superlative.

Examples: John is the tallest person in the class.
Eric is the shortest person in the class.
The highest mountain in the world is Mount Everest.

Adjectives of two syllables ending in *y* also add *est* to form the superlative.

Spelling Note   Two-syllable adjectives ending in *y* change the *y* to *i.*

Examples:
Laura is the prettiest student in the class.
Marie is the friendliest of all the students.

Irregular forms:

good–better–the best
bad–worse–the worst

Practice A   Work with a partner. Fill in this chart about the people in your class.

<table>
<tr><td></td><td>NAME</td><td></td><td>SUPERLATIVE</td></tr>
<tr><td>Example: Sam</td><td></td><td>is the</td><td>tallest student in the class.</td></tr>
<tr><td></td><td></td><td>tall</td><td></td></tr>
<tr><td></td><td></td><td>short</td><td></td></tr>
<tr><td></td><td></td><td>young</td><td></td></tr>
<tr><td></td><td></td><td>old</td><td></td></tr>
<tr><td></td><td></td><td>heavy</td><td></td></tr>
<tr><td></td><td></td><td>strong</td><td></td></tr>
<tr><td></td><td></td><td>loud</td><td></td></tr>
<tr><td></td><td></td><td>quiet</td><td></td></tr>
</table>

NAME		SUPERLATIVE
_____	friendly	_____
_____	kind	_____
_____	neat	_____
_____	fast	_____
_____	happy	_____
_____	smart	_____

Practice B   Work with a group. Answer these questions. The teacher will ask you to report your group's answers. Here are some expressions to use when you are stating your opinion:

> I think that . . .
> I'm pretty sure that . . .
> In my opinion . . .
> I'm not sure but I think . . .

What is the longest river in the world? _____

What is the highest mountain in the world? _____

What is the biggest country in the world? _____

What is the largest city in the world? _____

What is the largest waterfall in the world? _____

What is the longest mountain range in the world? _____

What is the oldest city in the world? _____

What is the fastest vehicle in the world? _____

What is the hardest material in the world? _____

What is the hottest place in the world? _____

What is the coldest place in the world? _____

What is the biggest animal in the world? _____

What is the smallest animal in the world? _____

What is the smartest animal in the world? _____

What is the prettiest country in the world? _____

What is the cleanest city in the world? _____

What is the best food in the world? _____

What is the easiest language in the world? _____

Who are the friendliest people in the world? _____

Make your own statements with superlatives.

_____

_____

_____

Lesson 10   INFINITIVES

Explanation   Some verbs require an infinitive. The infinitive is the verb form with *to*.

Examples: want **to** . . .   We want to buy a car.
She wants to take another course.
Do you want to get some coffee?

would like **to** . . . He would like to take a trip.
We'd like to leave early.
Would you like to learn a song?

Other verbs requiring infinitives:

need **to** . . .	She needs to study more.
plan **to** . . .	He plans to get a job.
decide **to** . . .	They're deciding to move.
agree **to** . . .	He agrees to pay for the wine.
promise **to** . . .	Do you promise to do your homework?
try **to** . . .	Is he trying to find a job?
remember **to** . . .	Remember to turn off the lights.
forget **to** . . .	Don't forget to turn off the lights.

Practice A   What three things do you want to do this weekend? Get the same information from your partner.

MY WEEKEND   MY PARTNER'S WEEKEND

1. _____   _____

2. _____   _____

3. _____   _____

Practice B   Talk to as many people as possible. Ask these questions:

> What do you want to do on your next holiday?
> What do you plan to do when you finish this course?

	NAME	NEXT HOLIDAY	AFTER THIS COURSE
1.			
2.			
3.			
4.			
5.			
6.			
7.			
8.			
9.			
10.			
11.			
12.			
13.			
14.			
15.			

Write about two of your classmates.

1. _____   2. _____

Practice C   Answer these questions by yourself.
Write down two places you'd like to visit.

1. _____

2. _____

Write down two things you'd like to do in your life.

1. _____

2. _____

Write down two people you'd like to meet.

1. _____

2. _____

Walk around and talk to as many people as possible. Ask these questions:

| What place would you like to visit? |
| Who would you like to meet? |
| What would you like to do in your life? |

	NAME	PLACE	PERSON	ACCOMPLISHMENT
1.				
2.				
3.				
4.				
5.				
6.				
7.				
8.				
9.				
10.				
11.				
12.				
13.				
14.				
15.				

Lesson 11 INFINITIVES

Explanation   There are many ways to express necessity. One of these is *need to . . .*

Practice A   With a partner, state what these people need to do.

1. Adam's thirsty. _____ *He needs to drink something.* _____

2. Anne and Laura are hungry. _____

3. Amanda's got a headache. _____

4. Mary Ann has a toothache. _____

5. Robert's rent is too high. _____

6. Rebecca's phone is out of order. _____

7. Jessica's got the flu. _____

8. Charlie's computer isn't working. _____

9. Rachel has a sore ankle. _____

10. Allan's overweight. _____

11. Stephanie is very lonely. _____

12. John and Ryan's apartment is messy. _____

13. Maureen is very sick. _____

14. Daniel's got a cough. _____

Practice B   What are two problems you have?

1. _____

2. _____

What do you need to do?

1. _____

2. _____

What are two problems your partner has?

1. _____

2. _____

What does your partner need to do?

1. _____

2. _____

Practice C   Work with a partner. Read this, and answer the questions.

The High Cost of Travel

If you would like to travel, and you want to visit some of the world's biggest cities, you need to take plenty of money with you. These are the costs of visiting some world cities:

CITY	RESTAURANT	HOTEL	SHORT STAY
Chicago	$31	$292	$420
Hong Kong	$46	$185	$334
London	$35	$477	$643
Los Angeles	$19	$173	$280
Mexico City	$26	$239	$238
Montreal	$26	$233	$360
New York	$40	$300	$473
Paris	$25	$173	$268
São Paulo	$17	$258	$361
Singapore	$26	$140	$250
Tokyo	$128	$286	$742
Toronto	$26	$227	$348

Restaurant Cost: Price of dinner for one—sirloin or rump steak, vegetable, potato, dessert plus service in a good restaurant (drinks not included).

Hotel Cost: Price of a double room with private bath and toilet, including breakfast and service in a first-class hotel.

Short Stay Cost: Cost of two evening meals with wine, overnight stay for two, car rental for 100 km. or public transportation and taxi, as well as smaller items such as color film and a telephone call.

What city has the highest hotel prices? _____

Which city has the lowest hotel prices? _____

Which city has the highest restaurant prices? _____

Which city has the cheapest restaurant prices? _____

Which is the cheapest Asian city for a short trip? _____

Which is the cheapest American city to visit for a short stay? _____

Compare the cost of a short stay in Toronto and Paris.

_____

Compare restaurant costs in São Paulo and Mexico City.

_____

Compare hotel costs in Tokyo and New York.

_____

How much do two people need to spend for a short stay in Los Angeles? _____

How much do two people need to spend for dinner in Hong Kong? _____

How much do two people need to spend for an overnight stay in Singapore? _____

Lesson 12   REQUESTS

Explanation   We use structures such as *I'd like to . . . I want to . . .* to make requests.
Here are some ways of making requests.

Could I . . .	Could I cash a check?	directness
I'd like to . . .	I'd like to cash a check.	of
I want to . . .	I want to cash a check.	request
I need to . . .	I need to cash a check.	increases

Practice A   Work with a partner. What do you sometimes need to do at the bank? Please circle.

see the manager	deposit some money
open an account	close an account
withdraw some money	fill out a change of address
buy a money order	get the balance
certify a check	cash a check
put a stop payment on a check	buy traveler's checks
exchange foreign currency	get a printout of recent checks
apply for a bank card	apply for a loan

OTHER _____

Write out five requests.

1. _____

2. _____

3. _____

4. _____

5. _____

Explanation   As you know, we make requests in different ways. The grammatical structure we use depends on the situation and how well we know the other person. We use formal requests when we talk to strangers. We use less formal requests when we talk to classmates, coworkers, and friends. We use direct commands only when we talk to very close friends, to family members, or to small children.

Examples: Formal:
Would you please open the door?
Could you please open the door?

Less Formal:
Would you open the door?
Could you open the door?
Please open the door.
Can you open the door?

Direct:
Open the door.

Practice A   Work with a partner. What are some requests you need to make? Where do you make requests?

PLACE: AT SCHOOL   PLACE: AT HOME   PLACE: _____

_____   _____   _____

_____   _____   _____

_____   _____   _____

_____   _____   _____

Practice B   With a partner, restate these commands.

Examples 1. Open the window.   Formal: _Would you please open the window?_

Less formal: _Can you open the window?_

2. Turn the music down.   Formal: _____

Less formal: _____

3. Turn the television on.   Formal: _____

Less formal: _____

4. Look this word up.   Formal: _____

Less formal: _____

5. Wait for us.   Formal: _____

Less formal: _____

6. Turn the lights off.

Formal: _____

Less formal: _____

7. Say that again.

Formal: _____

Less formal: _____

8. Explain this word to me.

Formal: _____

Less formal: _____

9. Spell your name for me.

Formal: _____

Less formal: _____

10. Call the security guard.

Formal: _____

Less formal: _____

Lesson 14   THE USE OF *WANT SOMEONE TO*

Explanation

To make a very direct request we use a command. The structure: *want . . . to* also expresses a very direct request.

Examples:

COMMAND	*WANT SOMEONE TO*
Clean up your room.	I want you to clean up your room.
Pay attention.	I want you to pay attention.
Listen to me.	I want you to listen to me.

This structure can also report a request.

Examples: Marie **wants David to pick** her up after work.
The girls **want the boys to dance** with them.
He **wants us to come** early.

Practice A

What do you want the teacher of this class to do? Circle.

give more homework   speak slowly   speak loudly

correct your mistakes   read more stories   do more exercises

take the class on a trip   practice more conversation

OTHER _____

Write out one important request.

_____

What do you want your classmates to do? Circle.

come to class on time   stop talking in class   be friendlier

talk more in class   speak louder   get together after class

OTHER _____

Write out one important request.

_____

Practice B   Walk around and ask your classmates these questions:

> What do you want the teacher of this class to do?
> What do you want your classmates to do?
> What do you want the principal of this school to do?

NAME	TEACHER	CLASSMATES	PRINCIPAL
1.			
2.			
3.			
4.			
5.			
6.			
7.			
8.			
9.			
10.			
11.			
12.			
13.			
14.			
15.			

Report the three most interesting answers to the class.

1. _____

2. _____

3. _____

Practice C   Talk to your partner. Discuss what you **don't want** people to do.

	ME	MY PARTNER
Best friend:	_____	_____
Husband/Wife or Boyfriend/Girlfriend:	_____	_____
Teacher:	_____	_____
Other students:	_____	_____

Practice D   Work with a partner. Report the messages in these notes. Use *want someone to . . .* in the answers.

1.
> Jessica:
>
> Please meet me at Yorkdale Shopping Center at 7 P.M. tonight.
>
> Justin

_____ *Justin wants Jessica to meet him at Yorkdale Shopping Center at 7.* _____.

2.
> Ryan:
>
> Pick up some bread and milk on your way home.
>
> Rachel

_____

3.
> Laura:
>
> Please lend me your car for the weekend.
>
> Adam

_____

4.
James:
Take out the garbage.
Eric and Joe

5.
Rebecca:
Drop off my sweater at the cleaners.
Thomas

6.
Linda and Amanda:
Please don't wait for me after school.
Michelle

7.
Matthew and Marie:
Please lock the door and leave the key under the mat.
David and Steven

8.
Ms. Reid:
Please mail our grades to our home addresses as soon as possible. Thanks,
Daniel and Robert

---

9.   Emily:

Don't forget to buy a birthday gift for Alex.

Alex

---

10.   Steven:

Don't smoke when we aren't at home.

Mom and Dad

---

11.   Jennifer:

Please call Dr. Ross A.S.A.P.

Kevin

---

12.   Emily:

Remember this Friday is a very special day.

Alex

---

13.   Joshua:

Don't touch this cake. It's for a surprise birthday party.

Emily and Sarah

14.
> Nick and Joe:
>
> Don't park in the driveway on Saturday morning.
> We're expecting a delivery truck.
>
> Vicky and Sam

Write your own note:

15.

Lesson 15 REVIEW OF TENSES

Practice A. The Airport

With a partner, use the correct tense and the correct form of the verb in this story.

The San Francisco International Airport (not be) _____ far from downtown San Francisco. It usually (take) _____ less than half an hour to drive there. There (be) _____ three terminals at the airport, the South Terminal, the North Terminal, and the International Terminal. These (always be) _____ busy. On any one day, flights (arrive) _____ from and (take) _____ off for destinations all over the world. A plane (land) _____ every few minutes. Planes (take) _____ off just as often.

Today, the arrivals section of the International Terminal (be) _____ especially crowded. Several flights (come) _____ in from Asia and Europe. Many people (wait) _____ to pick up friends and relatives. Some (hold) _____ up signs. Others (try) _____ to get near the glass partitions because they want (catch) _____ sight of their relatives.

The departures section (not be) _____ as busy at this moment. Only a few passengers (line) _____ up to go through the security checks. Some people (hug) _____ and (kiss) _____ good-bye. One older woman (have got) _____ tears in her eyes. She (carry) _____ a bouquet of roses. She (say) _____ good-bye to her children and grandchildren. She (leave) _____ the U.S.A. for good.

People (have) _____ so many different emotions at this airport. They (feel) _____ both happy and sad here. They (be) _____ happy when they (go) _____ away on vacation or when they (meet) _____ loved ones. They (feel) _____ sad when they (leave) _____ home or (see) _____ people off.

The airport itself (not look) _____ like a very emotional place. It (not have) _____ anything unusual about it. It (look) _____ cold, modern, and efficient. But on any given day this airport (see) _____ more emotions than any place else in San Francisco.

Practice B. *Getting a New Telephone*

With a partner, use the correct tense and the correct form of the verb.

Tim: Hi, Emily, how (go) _____ it _____ ?

Emily: I (have got) _____ a big problem. I (have) _____ a new place, and I need (get) _____ a telephone right away.

Tim: That (not be) _____ a problem. The telephone company (have) _____ stores and offices all over the city.

Emily: (think) _____ you _____ that it (be) _____ as easy as that? A person just (walk) _____ in and (get) _____ a phone?

Tim: There (be) _____ nothing easier. When you (get) _____ to the phone company store, first you (fill) _____ out an application form with your new address. Then you (give) _____ the form to the clerk. The clerk (enter) _____ all the information into the computer.

Emily: (be) _____ that all? (come) _____ someone _____ to install the telephone?

Tim: I (not think) _____ so. You probably (have) _____ telephone jacks in your apartment.

Emily: I (not understand) _____. How (get) _____ I _____ the phone?

Tim: You (do) _____ that in the store. The clerk (ask) _____ you to choose a phone. You (pick) _____ out the style and the color. Then they (get) _____ it from the stockroom. The clerk (put) _____ it into a box and (give) _____ it to you. You (take) _____ the phone home and (plug) _____ it in.

Emily: How much (cost) _____ the phone _____ ? (need) _____ I _____ (pay) _____ for it right away?

Tim: (not worry) _____. The telephone company always (get) _____ its money. They always (bill) _____ you. They (not require)

_____ usually _____ immediate payment. Sometimes if you are a new

customer, they (ask) _____ for a deposit.

Emily: That (sound) _____ simple. I (go) _____ to the telephone store

right away. (want) _____ you _____ to come with me?

Tim: There (be) _____ one in the shopping mall down the street. Steven and I

(drive) _____ there now. Let's (go) _____ together.

Functioning in Conversation

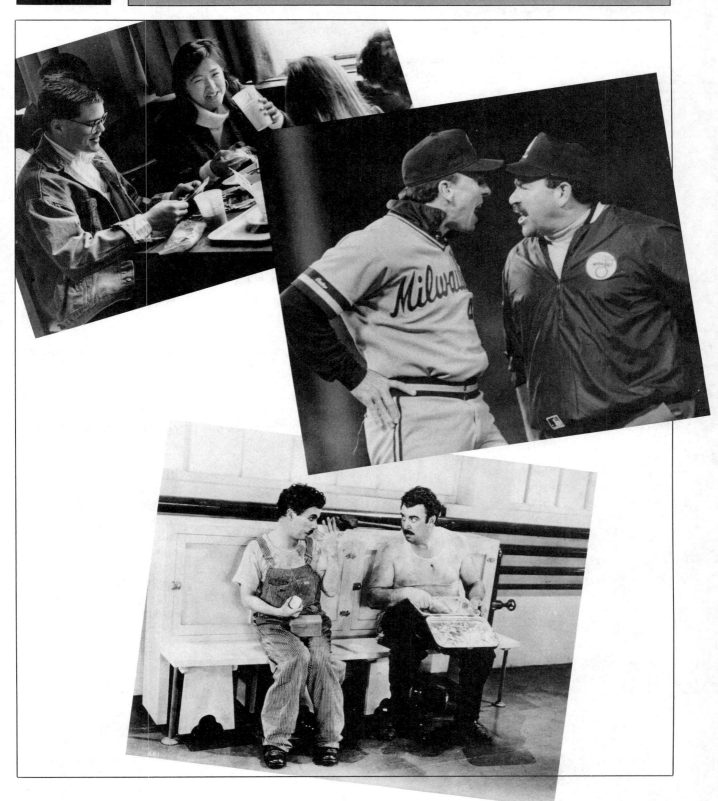

Explanation　　We form the **regular past tense** by adding *ed* to the verb stem.

> **Examples:**　wanted　　　answered　　　liked
> 　　　　　　　needed　　　stayed　　　　jumped

Most verbs in English are regular.
We pronounce the past tense ending as *ed* **only** when the verb ends in *t* or *d*.

> **Examples:**　wanted　needed　added　subtracted　rented　landed

We pronounce the past tense ending *ed* as *d* when the verb ends in a voiced sound.

> **Examples:**　smiled　grinned　answered　called　opened　swallowed

We pronounce the past tense ending *ed* as *t* when the verb ends in a voiceless consonant.

> **Examples:**　talked　danced　pushed　watched　laughed　stopped

Spelling Note　　If a verb ends in *y* and the letter before it is a consonant, change the *y* to *i*.

> study　　studied
> hurry　　hurried

If the verb ends in a single vowel followed by a single consonant, double the consonant.

> stop　　stopped

Practice A　　Work with a partner. Write the **past tense** of the verbs and categorize them according to the pronunciation of the past tense ending.

live	smoke	like
study	press	sneeze
work	try	cough
stop	cook	choke
finish	boil	call
bake	turn	play
kick	fry	shave
push	kiss	wash
slap	comb	hug
cry	clean	scream
look	brush	believe
close	mix	listen
love	walk	stay
	breathe	

ED PRONOUNCED AS T

_____ _____ _____ _____

_____ _____ _____ _____

_____ _____ _____ _____

_____ _____ _____ _____

_____ _____ _____ _____

ED PRONOUNCED AS D

_____ _____ _____ _____

_____ _____ _____ _____

_____ _____ _____ _____

_____ _____ _____ _____

Lesson 2   PAST TENSE OF REGULAR VERBS

Explanation   These are the forms of the **past tense**:

AFFIRMATIVE	INTERROGATIVE	WITH QUESTION WORDS
I worked	Did I work?	Why did I work?
you studied	Did you study?	What did you study?
we finished	Did we finish?	When did we finish?
they cleaned	Did they clean?	What did they clean?
he watched	Did he watch?	What did he watch?
she cooked	Did she cook?	What did she cook?
it ended	Did it end?	When did it end?
John answered	Did John answer?	What did John answer?

NEGATIVE	CONTRACTIONS
I did not work	I didn't work
you did not study	you didn't study
we did not finish	we didn't finish
they did not clean	they didn't clean
he did not watch	he didn't watch
she did not cook	she didn't cook
it did not end	it didn't end
John did not answer	John didn't answer

These time expressions require the use of the past tense:

last night	**yesterday**	two days **ago**
last year	**before**	many years **ago**

Practice A   What did you do this morning? What did you do yesterday evening? Here are some verbs to use:

MORNING ROUTINE	YESTERDAY EVENING
brush	study
rinse	call
wash	watch
comb	cook
dress	wash
listen	clean

Example:

This morning I **brushed** my teeth. Then I **rinsed** my mouth. After that I **washed.** Then I **combed** my hair. After that I **listened** to the radio.

Write about you. Then get the same information from your partner.

ME

THIS MORNING   YESTERDAY EVENING

_____   _____

_____   _____

_____   _____

_____   _____

_____   _____

MY PARTNER

THIS MORNING   YESTERDAY EVENING

_____   _____

_____   _____

_____   _____

_____   _____

_____   _____

Practice B   Walk around and talk to as many classmates possible. Ask these questions:

> Where did you live three years ago?
> When did you arrive here?
> What was your first impression? Did you like it here?
> Why did you like it? **or** Why didn't you like it?

	NAME	PREVIOUS RESIDENCE	DATE OF ARRIVAL	FIRST IMPRESSION	REASON
1.					
2.					
3.					
4.					
5.					

	NAME	PREVIOUS RESIDENCE	DATE OF ARRIVAL	FIRST IMPRESSION	REASON
6.					
7.					
8.					
9.					
10.					
11.					
12.					
13.					
14.					
15.					

Practice C   With a partner, read the story and underline the verbs. Then retell this story in the **past tense.**

Grant's Paradise Grill

Grant Palmer lives in Miami Beach. He lives in Florida because he doesn't like cold weather, and he absolutely hates snow and ice and freezing temperatures. He doesn't have a perfect life but he's happy. Grant owns a small restaurant. He works from early in the morning to late at night.

His schedule is tiring. First, early in the morning, Grant shops for food at the markets. He looks for the freshest seafood and vegetables. Then he plans the menu. He cooks the daily specials, and often bakes pies and cakes, too. Grant changes the menu every day.

The grill opens at lunchtime. Customers arrive a little early, and sometimes they line up to get a table. They love Grant's food, and they order a lot of it. Grant talks to his customers because he enjoys his work.

Grant doesn't charge a lot, and he doesn't make a lot of money. Another problem is that Grant is always tired when he closes up late at night. But the biggest problem is that Grant wants to spend more time on the love of his life: sailing.

Grant's Paradise Grill

Five years ago, _____

_____

_____

_____

_____

_____

_____

_____

_____

_____

With your partner, ask questions in the past tense about Grant.

Where (live) _____ Grant _____ before he moved to Miami Beach?

How long (own) _____ Grant _____ the restaurant?

Why (work) _____ he _____ so hard?

Why (shop) _____ he _____ for food every day?

How many courses (cook) _____ Grant _____?

Why (change) _____ he _____ the menu on a daily basis?

What kind of food (cook) _____ Grant _____?

How much food (order) _____ the customers _____?

How long (wait) _____ they _____?

What time (close) _____ the restaurant _____?

What (happen) _____ to Grant's Paradise Grill?

Practice D. Tense Review: Smoking

With a partner, use the correct form of the verb in these sentences. Use the **simple present** or the **past** or the **present progressive tense.**

1. Ed (smoke)_____*smokes*_____ a package of cigarettes every week.

2. He (start) _____ to smoke when he (be) _____ a teenager.

3. He (try) _____ to stop now because he (know) _____ it (not be) _____ healthy to smoke.

4. Victoria (be) _____ Ed's girlfriend.

5. Every day she (tell) _____ him that smoking (be) _____ bad for him.

6. She also (smoke) _____ three years ago, but then she (stop) _____ .

7. Last winter Ed (look) _____ very unhealthy.

8. At that time, he (cough) _____ and (sneeze) _____ all the time.

9. He also (need) _____ to rest very often.

10. Last winter Ed (smoke) _____ over a package of cigarettes every day.

11. The nurse at his school (warn) _____ him that smoking (cause) _____ many illnesses.

12. Ed (decide) _____ to listen to the nurse, and he (try) _____ to stop.

13. He (not be) _____ successful the first time he (stop) _____ .

14. His willpower (grow) _____ stronger now.

15. He (count) _____ the number of cigarettes he (smoke) _____ every day.

16. He (want) _____ to give up smoking completely by next summer.

Lesson 3 PAST TENSE OF IRREGULAR VERBS

Explanation   These are the forms of the **past tense:**

AFFIRMATIVE	QUESTION FORM	WITH QUESTION WORDS
I ate	Did I eat?	What did I eat?
you drank	Did you drink?	What did you drink?
we had	Did we have?	What did we have?
they met	Did they meet?	Who did they meet?
he went	Did he go?	Where did he go?
she spoke	Did she speak?	How did she speak?
it said	Did it say?	What did it say?

NEGATIVE	CONTRACTIONS
I did not eat	I didn't eat
you did not drink	you didn't drink
we did not have	we didn't have
they did not meet	they didn't meet
he did not go	he didn't go
she did not speak	she didn't speak
it did not say	it didn't say

These time expressions require the use of the past tense:

last week	two weeks **ago**	**yesterday**
last month	five months **ago**	
the **last** time	a little while **ago**	
last Saturday	the day **before**	

Practice A   Here are some irregular verbs:

go—went   speak—spoke
eat—ate   meet—met
drink—drank   have—had

With a partner, tell this story in the **past tense.**

1. Sarah often goes to parties on Saturday nights.

   Last Saturday Sarah went to a party.

2. She meets a lot of new people.

   _____

3. She eats interesting food.

   _____

4. She drinks a lot of wine.

   _____

5. She smokes a lot of cigarettes.

   _____

6. She dances to the lastest hit songs.

   _____

7. She speaks to some very interesting people.

   _____

8. She goes home quite late.

   _____

9. She has a good time, but she also has a headache the next morning.

   _____

Tell about the last party you went to.

_____

_____

_____

_____

_____

_____

Practice B   Here are some irregular verbs:

drive—drove	tell—told
pay—paid	give—gave
get—got	meet—met
take—took	make—made

With a partner, tell this story in the **past tense.**

1. Jerry drives a taxi on Saturday nights.

   Two years ago, Jerry drove a taxi on Saturday nights.

2. He meets a lot of different people.

3. They tell him many interesting stories.

4. He takes people all over the city.

5. Jerry gets a lot of passengers at the airport.

6. They pay their fares in cash.

7. They usually give him small tips as well.

8. Jerry drives for eight hours on Saturdays.

_____

9. He makes good money driving a cab.

_____

Tell about a job you had in the past.

_____

_____

_____

_____

_____

Practice C   Here are some past tense verbs:

take—took   get—got
teach—taught   speak—spoke
read—read   write—wrote
have—had   make—made
spend—spent   understand—understood

With a partner, tell this story in the **past tense.**

1. Stephanie takes a Spanish course on Monday evenings.

   Last year, Stephanie took a Spanish course on Monday evenings.

2. She gets to school at 7 P.M.

   _____

3. The teacher teaches until 8 P.M.

   _____

4. Then the class takes a short break.

   _____

5. The students speak Spanish during the break.

   _____

6. Afterwards they read Spanish stories.

   _____

7. Sometimes they write Spanish sentences on the board.

_____

8. The students have a good time at class.

_____

9. They make friends with each other.

_____

10. Most of the students understand a lot of Spanish.

_____

11. They spend a great deal of time speaking Spanish.

_____

Tell about a course you took in the past.

_____

_____

_____

_____

_____

Practice D   Talk to as many people in the class as possible. Ask these questions:

> What did you do last Saturday night?
> Were you alone?
> Did you have a good time?

	NAME	ACTIVITY	WITH WHOM?	GOOD TIME?
1.				
2.				
3.				
4.				
5.				
6.				
7.				

NAME	ACTIVITY	WITH WHOM?	GOOD TIME?
8. _____			
9. _____			
10. _____			
11. _____			
12. _____			
13. _____			
14. _____			
15. _____			

Practice E   Talk to as many classmates as possible. Use this conversation:

First partner: Hello, _____ . May I ask you some questions?

Second partner: Of course. Go ahead.

First partner: When did you come here?

Second partner: I came here _____ .

First partner: What did you do before you came here?

Second partner: _____

First partner: How did you get here?

Second partner: _____

Possible answers to, "What did you do before you came here?":

I made an application.
I got a visa.
I had a medical check-up.
I had an interview.
I got a job.

_____

_____

Possible answers to, "How did you get here?":

I took a plane from _____.

I flew to New York, and then _____.

_____

	NAME	DATE OF ARRIVAL	TWO THINGS BEFORE COMING HERE	HOW
1.				
2.				
3.				
4.				
5.				
6.				
7.				
8.				
9.				
10.				
11.				
12.				
13.				
14.				
15.				

Report two of the most interesting answers to the class:

_____

_____

Explanation   Here are the past tense forms of the most common irregular verbs in English:

SIMPLE FORM	PAST FORM	SIMPLE FORM	PAST FORM
be	was, were	learn	learnt (learned)
become	became	leave	left
begin	began	lend	lent
bite	bit	let	let
blow	blew	lie	lay
break	broke	lose	lost
bring	brought	make	made
build	built	mean	meant
burn	burnt (burned)	meet	met
buy	bought	put	put
catch	caught	read	read
choose	chose	ride	rode
come	came	run	ran
cost	cost	say	said
cut	cut	see	saw
do	did	sell	sold
draw	drew	send	sent
dream	dreamt (dreamed)	set	set
drink	drank	shoot	shot
drive	drove	sing	sang
eat	ate	sit	sat
fall	fell	sleep	slept
feel	felt	smell	smelt (smelled)
fight	fought	speak	spoke
find	found	spend	spent
fly	flew	spread	spread
forget	forgot	stand	stood
get	got	steal	stole
give	gave	stick	stuck
go	went	swim	swam
grow	grew	take	took
hang	hung	teach	taught
have	had	tear	tore
hear	heard	tell	told
hide	hid	think	thought
hold	held	throw	threw
hurt	hurt	understand	understood
keep	kept	wake	woke
know	knew	wear	wore
lead	led	win	won
		write	wrote

Practice A   With a partner, find the past tense forms for these verbs.

give _____   break _____   get _____

have _____   make _____   lend _____

tell _____   catch _____   take _____

buy _____   forget _____   hear _____

By yourself, answer these questions.

When did you last catch a cold? _____

When did you last take pictures? _____

When did you last make a long distance call? _____

When did you last break something? _____

When did you last buy something? _____

When did you last get sick? _____

When did you last have a headache? _____

When did you last forget something? _____

When did you last give someone a gift? _____

When did you last lend someone some money? _____

When did you last tell a lie? _____

When did you last hear the news? _____

Work with a partner. Ask your partner any three of these questions, but get one more piece of information.

Examples: A: When did you last hear the news?
B: I heard the news yesterday evening.
A: What station did you hear it on?
B: I heard it on WRNO.

A: When did you last write a letter?
B: I wrote a letter last Thursday.
B: Who did you write the letter to?
A: I wrote it to my cousin in Korea.

When you finish, find another partner and ask three more questions. The teacher will ask you to report to the class.

	PARTNER #1	PARTNER #2
1.	_____	_____
	_____	_____
2.	_____	_____
	_____	_____
3.	_____	_____
	_____	_____

Practice B   With a partner, find the past tense forms for these verbs.

sing _____   sleep _____   speak _____

lose _____   make _____   ride _____

send _____   write _____   see _____

go _____   eat _____   wear _____

Answer these questions by yourself.

When did you last go out for dinner? _____

When did you last see a movie? _____

When did you last speak to your best friend? _____

When did you last send a card? _____

When did you last eat "junk food"? _____

When did you last write an examination? _____

When did you last wear a bathing suit? _____

When did you last lose your temper? _____

When did you last make a big mistake? _____

When did you last sleep in? _____

When did you last sing a song? _____

When did you last ride a bicycle? _____

Ask a partner three of these questions, but get more information. When you finish, find another partner and ask three more questions. The teacher will ask you to report to the class.

PARTNER #1   PARTNER #2

1. _____   _____

   _____   _____

2. _____   _____

   _____   _____

3. _____   _____

   _____   _____

Practice C. Jennifer's Weekend

Work with a partner. Use the correct past tense forms of the verbs in this story.

Jennifer (be) _____ a student at Mohawk College in Albany, New York. Last weekend she (have) _____ an assignment and an essay to do. She (plan) _____ to (work) _____ at the library all weekend. On Saturday morning, she (get) _____ an early start and (do) _____ some work. Then she (run) _____ into some old friends at the library. Over coffee she (find) _____ out that they (plan) _____ to (go) _____ skiing at their family's cottage near Lake Placid. They (invite) _____ Jennifer to (come) _____ along with them. She (feel) _____ guilty, but she (agree) _____. They (leave) _____ Saturday afternoon. They (drive) _____ to Lake Placid. They (get) _____ to the mountains by four o'clock and (ski) _____ until late at night. That evening, more friends (come) _____ to the cottage. They (bring) _____ a lot of food. Jennifer and her friends (have) _____ a late supper and later they all (go) _____ to a discotheque. Everyone (laugh) _____ and (tell)

_____ jokes and (sing) _____ songs. They (spend) _____ the next day skiing, and later they (eat) _____ lunch at a charming country inn. Jennifer (get) _____ back to Albany late Sunday evening. She (have) _____ a wonderful time, but she (feel) _____ very guilty about not doing her work.

Ask Jennifer some questions. Use these question words.

What _____ *What did you do on the weekend?* _____

Where _____

How _____

How long _____

What kind of _____

Why _____

How much _____

What _____

Whose _____

When _____

How many _____

Practice D Walk around and talk to as many people as possible. Ask them:

> What did you do on the weekend?
> Where did you go?
> Did you enjoy yourself?

	NAME	ACTIVITY	LOCATION	ENJOY YOURSELF?
1.				
2.				
3.				
4.				
5.				
6.				

NAME	ACTIVITY	LOCATION	ENJOY YOURSELF?
7.			
8.			
9.			
10.			
11.			
12.			
13.			
14.			
15.			

Practice E. A Bad Day

With a partner, use the correct form of the verbs in this conversation.

Sarah and Michael work as tellers in different banks. They take English classes two nights a week. They often get together for coffee before class. This was their conversation last Monday evening before class.

Sarah: How (go) _____ your day _____ , Michael?

Michael: (not ask) _____ . Everything (go) _____ wrong today.

Sarah: What (happen) _____ today?

Michael: First of all I (sleep) _____ in. Then, I (get) _____ to work an hour late. My

boss (give) _____ me an angry look. Because I (be) _____ nervous, I

(forget) _____ to sign in on the time sheet. Next, I (make) _____ some

small mistakes with customers' deposits. One woman (get) _____ very angry. She (speak) _____ to the bank manager. At lunch, I (go) _____ to an expensive restaurant to try to relax. After I (order) _____ I (find) _____ that I (not have) _____ my wallet. I (not know) _____ what to do. I (run) _____ out red with embarrassment. Later the restaurant owner (come) _____ in to do some banking. I (think) _____ he (recognize) _____ me. I (make) _____ a big mistake with his deposit. He (blow) _____ up and (go) _____ to see the manager. I almost (lose) _____ my job. When I (get) _____ home, I (not have) _____ my keys. I (leave) _____ them at work.

Sarah: How (get) _____ you _____ in?

Michael: I (meet) _____ the superintendant and he (give) _____ me a spare set of keys. I (be) _____ glad this day (be) _____ almost over.

Sarah: Well, it (not be) _____ over yet. We (have) _____ the term test tonight.

Michael: Oh no! I (forget) _____ all about that.

Work with a partner. Explain why Michael had a bad day.

First, he _____

_____

Then, he _____

_____

After that, he _____

_____

Later, _____

_____

Finally, _____

_____

Practice F   Work with a partner. Think of a really bad day you had. Tell what happened. Then get the same information from your partner.

MY BAD DAY	MY PARTNER'S BAD DAY
_____	_____
_____	_____
_____	_____
_____	_____
_____	_____
_____	_____
_____	_____

Practice G   Answer these questions:

What was your last job? _____

What did you do? _____

What was your best job? _____

What did you do? _____

What was your worst job? _____

What did you do? _____

Talk to as many classmates as possible. Ask these questions.

> What was your best job?
> What did you do?
> What was your worst job?
> What did you do?

	NAME	BEST JOB	ACTIVITY	WORST JOB	ACTIVITY
1.					
2.					
3.					
4.					
5.					
6.					

	NAME	BEST JOB	ACTIVITY	WORST JOB	ACTIVITY
7.					
8.					
9.					
10.					
11.					
12.					
13.					
14.					
15.					

Tell the class about two of the best jobs and two of the worst jobs.

BEST JOBS   WORST JOBS

_____   _____

_____   _____

Practice H   List three things you did on your last vacation:

1. _____

2. _____

3. _____

Talk to as many people in the clasroom as possible. Ask these questions:

> Where did you go on your last vacation?
> What did you do?
> Did you have a good time?

	NAME	LOCATION	ACTIVITY	GOOD TIME?
1.				
2.				
3.				
4.				
5.				
6.				

	NAME	LOCATION	ACTIVITY	GOOD TIME?
7.				
8.				
9.				
10.				
11.				
12.				
13.				
14.				
15.				

Who do you think had the best vacation? _____

Lesson 5 — PAST TENSE: NEGATIVES

These are the forms of the negative.

AFFIRMATIVE	NEGATIVE	CONTRACTIONS
I went	I did not go	I didn't go
you came	you did not come	you didn't come
we ate	we did not eat	we didn't eat
they got	they did not get	they didn't get
he drank	he did not drink	he didn't drink
she bought	she did not buy	she didn't buy
it took	it did not take	it didn't take
Linda saw	Linda did not see	Linda didn't see

Practice A — With a partner, read about Mary Anne and write negatives about Melissa.

Mary Anne and her friend Melissa visited Mexico last year. They are close friends, but they are opposites in personality. Melissa didn't do any of the things Mary Anne did.

MARY ANNE'S TRIP	MELISSA'S TRIP

Mary Anne liked the beach. _____ *Melissa didn't like the beach.* _____

Mary Anne brought a lot of bathing suits. _____

Mary Anne went to the beach every day. _____

Mary Anne got a sun tan. _____

Mary Anne met people from all over the world. _____

Mary Anne took a lot of pictures. _____

Mary Anne visited all the sights. _____

Mary Anne learned some Spanish. _____

Mary Anne bought a lot of souvenirs. _____

Mary Anne went out for supper every night. _____

Mary Anne ate Mexican food. _____

Mary Anne drank Mexican drinks. _____

Mary Anne danced to Mexican music. _____

Mary Anne sent a lot of postcards. _____

Mary Anne had a wonderful time. _____

Mary Anne wanted to go back to Mexico. _____

Melissa didn't enjoy the trip as much as Mary Anne did. Melissa is sorry that she didn't do more things. What do you think she regrets?

Example: _____ *She's really sorry she didn't go to the beach more often.* _____

_____

_____

_____

_____

_____

We can use the expression *I'm sorry* + the **past tense** to express regrets about the past.

Examples: I'm sorry I didn't study more for the English test.
I'm sorry I spent so much time watching T.V.

Daniel's sorry he studied engineering.
He's sorry he didn't study medicine.

Marie's sorry she got married so young.
She's sorry she didn't get more education.

Practice A   Everyone has some regrets about the past.
Write one thing you are sorry you didn't do in the past in your studies or in your profession.

I'm sorry _____

Write one thing you are sorry you didn't do in your personal life.

I'm sorry _____

Talk to as many people in your class as possible. Get the same information.

NAME	REGRETS ABOUT STUDIES OR PROFESSION	REGRETS ABOUT PERSONAL LIFE
1.		
2.		
3.		
4.		
5.		
6.		
7.		
8.		
9.		
10.		
11.		
12.		

NAME	REGRETS ABOUT STUDIES OR PROFESSION	REGRETS ABOUT PERSONAL LIFE
13. ____		
14. ____		
15. ____		

<table></table>

Lesson 7	**REVIEW OF NEGATIVES**

Practice A   Work with a partner. Make negative sentences.

1. The class took a short break. _____ *The class didn't take a short break.* _____

2. Andrew ate meat. _____

3. They're smoking cigarettes. _____

4. Jane leaves at four o'clock. _____

5. You were very late. _____

6. Laura drives slowly. _____

7. Marie did the housework. _____

8. Our friends drank diet pop. _____

9. Sarah is talking to a student. _____

10. The customers were angry. _____

11. Michael lives downtown. _____

12. Jennifer took a taxi to school. _____

13. I like this course. _____

14. Mary Anne's buying groceries. _____

15. We do our shopping on Thursdays. _____

16. She's got a headache. _____

17. The passengers 're getting off the bus. _____

18. She threw out the papers. _____

19. Ellen's playing the piano. _____

20. They use the computer. _____

Lesson 8 | REFLEXIVE PRONOUNS

Explanation   These are the forms of the reflexive pronouns:

I	myself
you	yourself
he	himself
she	herself
it	itself
we	ourselves
you	yourselves
they	themselves

Examples: Marie hurt **herself.**
They did it **themselves.**
Henry smiled at **himself.**
We moved it by **ourselves.**

Practice A   With a partner answer these questions. Use reflexive pronouns.

1. Who did you hurt? (me) _____ *I hurt myself.* _____

2. Who did they scratch? (them) _____

3. Who did he burn? (him) _____

4. Who did she kick? (her) _____

5. Who did he cut? (him) _____

6. Who did you fool? (us) _____

7. Who did you make fun of? (us) _____

8. What did it see? (it) _____

9. Who did you laugh at? (me) _____

10. Who did you look at? (us) _____

11. Who did they frighten? (them) _____

Practice B   Work with a partner. Use reflexives in the sentences.

1. The children played alone. _____ *The children played by themselves.* _____

2. I went shopping alone. _____

3. Emily wrote the letter alone. _____

4. Did you make dinner without help? _____

5. Did you fix the car alone? (plural) _____

6. Did Kevin move the furniture without help? _____

7. They didn't do their homework without help. _____

8. Stephanie drove to New York alone. _____

9. Did you do the dishes alone? _____

10. Adam made the appointment alone. _____

11. Nicole did the housework alone. _____

12. We didn't have dinner alone. _____

Lesson 9   APOLOGIES

FORMAL APOLOGIES

I'm terribly sorry.
I'm awfully sorry.
Please excuse me.
I'm dreadfully sorry.
How clumsy of me.
How stupid of me.
Please forgive me.
I owe you an apology.

RESPONSES

That's quite all right.
It's quite all right.
Please don't worry about it.

We often put two of these expressions together.

Example: I'm terribly sorry. Please forgive me.

LESS FORMAL APOLOGIES

I'm sorry.
Sorry about that.
Excuse me.
Pardon me.
Sorry.

RESPONSES

That's all right.
It wasn't your fault.
I understand.
That's O.K.
Don't worry.
Not to worry.
No problem.
Forget about it.
You couldn't help it.
You didn't do it on purpose.

Example: A: I'm terribly sorry I broke your wine glass.
B: Please don't worry about it.
A: How clumsy of me. I don't usually break things.
B: That's all right. I'm sure you couldn't help it.

Practice A With a partner make apologies and responses in these situations. Then role play two of these situations.

1. You lost your friend's book.

   Apology: _____

   Response: _____

2. You forgot your friend's birthday.

   Apology: _____

   Response: _____

3. You came to your friend's party very late.

   Apology: _____

   Response: _____

4. You dialed the wrong number.

   Apology: _____

   Response: _____

5. You didn't invite your friend to your party.

   Apology: _____

   Response: _____

6. You spilled a glass of wine on your teacher's new carpet.

Apology: _____

Response: _____

7. You took your teacher's books by accident.

Apology: _____

Response: _____

8. You didn't do the shopping as you promised.

Apology: _____

Response: _____

9. You didn't clean up the kitchen.

Apology: _____

Response: _____

10. You bumped into a passenger on the subway.

Apology: _____

Response: _____

Lesson 10   COMMON RESPONSES

Explanation   People choose responses depending on the situation and how well they know each other.

Example:

SITUATION	STATEMENT	POSSIBLE RESPONSES
Thanking	Thank you.	You're welcome. That's all right. Don't mention it. Forget it.

A number of responses to a statement can be correct.

Practice A   Work with a partner. Match the responses to the statements.

EXPRESSION   RESPONSE

How do you do? ⟍   ⟋ Not too bad.

How are you? ⟋   ⟍ Pleased to meet you.

Congratulations!   Thank you. It was a gift.

Thank you!   You, too.

I'm awfully sorry!   You're welcome

Happy birthday!   Don't mention it.

Thank you!   Thank you.

Sorry about that!   Fine, thanks.

How's it going?   Don't worry about it.

What's new?   It's not your fault.

Good luck!   Not too much.

Have a nice day!   I'm afraid not.

See you later!   Thank you.

Do you have change for a dollar?   Thank you.

Lovely day!   Have a good day.

What a beautiful ring!   Just gorgeous!

Cold enough for you?   It's nice to meet you, too.

Glad to meet you.   Oh, yes. I hate the cold.

Lesson 11 | FUTURE TIME: THE PRESENT CONTINUOUS TENSE

Explanation   We can express future plans by using the present continuous tense with future time adverbials.
Future time expressions:
   tomorrow
   after school
   in a few minutes
   soon
   next week

Examples: We're having a test tomorrow.
They're going out after school.
I'm leaving in a few minutes.
She's getting married soon.
He's arriving next week.

Practice A   Talk to as many people as possible. Ask them:

> What are you doing after class today?
> What are you doing on the weekend?

	NAME	AFTER CLASS TODAY	THIS WEEKEND
1.			
2.			
3.			
4.			
5.			
6.			
7.			
8.			
9.			
10.			
11.			
12.			
13.			
14.			
15.			

What is the most interesting activity after school? _____

What is the most interesting activity on the weekend? _____

Lesson 12 FUTURE TIME: *TO BE GOING TO*

Explanation   *To be going to . . .* expresses intentions in the future.

AFFIRMATIVE

I am going to study
he is going to work
she is going to rest
it is going to rain
we are going to drive
you are going to leave
they are going to stay

CONTRACTIONS

I'm going to study
he's going to work
she's going to rest
it's going to rain
we're going to drive
you're going to leave
they're going to stay

QUESTION FORM	WITH QUESTION WORDS
Am I going to study?	What am I going to study?
Is he going to work?	Where is he going to work?
Is she going to rest?	When is she going to rest?
Is it going to rain?	When is it going to rain?
Are we going to drive?	Why are we going to drive?
Are you going to leave?	When are you going to leave?
Are they going to stay?	How long are they going to stay?

NEGATIVES	CONTRACTIONS
I am not going to study	I'm not going to study
he is not going to work	he isn't going to work
she is not going to rest	she isn't going to rest
it is not going to rain	it isn't going to rain
we are not going to drive	we aren't going to drive
you are not going to leave	you aren't going to leave
they are not going to stay	they aren't going to stay

In normal fast speech, in informal situations, *going to* is pronounced *"gonna"*.

I'm **gonna** go now.
He's **gonna** drive.
They're **gonna** study.

We do *not* usually use these forms in writing.

These future time adverbials require the use of the future tense:

tomorrow	**after** work	**on the weekend**
next month	**in** a little while	**soon**
next year	**in** a couple of days	

Practice A   Work with a partner. What do you think is going to happen in these situations? Make statements with *to be going to* and the verbs listed.

1. George is tired. (rest) _____ *George is going to rest.* _____

2. Ryan doesn't like his job. (look for) _____

3. The students are hungry. (have) _____

4. Ellen's car had a flat tire. (change) _____

5. Anne is overweight. (go on a diet) _____

6. Tim and Laura's VCR broke down. (buy) _____

7. Their apartment is too small. (move) _____

8. James lost his dictionary. (borrow) _____

9. Melissa's got a headache. (take) _____

10. She bought the wrong size shoes. (exchange) _____

11. Justin failed the last test. (study) _____

12. I forgot to send my friend a birthday card. (call up) _____

13. The athlete hurt himself. (take it easy) _____

14. Her husband said the wrong thing. (apologize) _____

15. David caught the flu. (stay) _____

16. They ran out of coffee. (get) _____

17. Matthew smokes too much. (cut down) _____

18. Emily took the wrong bus. (ask for) _____

Practice B   What are two problems you have right now?

1. _____

2. _____

What are you going to do?

1. _____

2. _____

Talk to as many people as possible. Ask each person about a problem they have, and what they are going to do about it.

	NAME	PROBLEM	SOLUTION
1.			
2.			
3.			
4.			
5.			
6.			
7.			
8.			
9.			
10.			
11.			
12.			

	NAME	PROBLEM	SOLUTION
13.			
14.			
15.			

Practice C   What are you are going to do when your English is fluent?

_____

_____

Talk to as many classmates as possible. Get the same information.

	NAME	INTENTIONS
1.		
2.		
3.		
4.		
5.		
6.		
7.		
8.		
9.		
10.		
11.		
12.		
13.		
14.		
15.		

What are most people going to do when their English is fluent?

_____

Practice D   Work with a partner. Make questions with *to be going to.*

1. They had a party last week. _____*Are they going to have a party next week?*_____

2. They invited all the students to their last party. _____

_____

3. The teachers went on strike last year. _____

_____

4. James worked overtime last week. _____

_____

5. They took a trip to Florida last winter. _____

_____

6. We were late yesterday. _____

_____

7. The weather was cold last winter. _____

_____

8. Melissa did the laundry last week. _____

_____

9. They drove to school last week. _____

_____

10. Eric and Dan had supper at a restaurant yesterday. _____

_____

11. They taught in Japan several years ago. _____

_____

12. We got tickets for a concert last month. _____

_____

13. The photographer took a class picture last year. _____

_____

14. We made a lot of mistakes on the last test. _____

_____

15. The last examination was very difficult. _____

_____

Practice E   Imagine this is the end of the English course for your class. You are going to have a party to celebrate. Work with a partner. Ask questions about the party.

Where _____ ?

When _____ ?

What kind of food _____ ?

What kind of music _____ ?

What kind of drinks _____ ?

What time _____ ?

How _____ ?

What kind of clothes _____ ?

How many _____ ?

How much _____ ?

How long _____ ?

Who _____ ?

What _____ ?

Think of three other questions to ask.

1. _____

2. _____

3. _____

Lesson 13 | FUTURE TIME: _WILL_

Explanation   We use either _to be going to_ . . . or _will_ . . . to make predictions about the future.

AFFIRMATIVE	CONTRACTIONS	QUESTION FORM
I will work	I'll work	Will I work?
you will study	you'll study	Will you study?
he will come	he'll come	Will he come?
she will go	she'll go	Will she go?
we will write	we'll write	Will we write?
they will read	they'll read	Will they read?

NEGATIVES	CONTRACTIONS
I will not work	I won't work
you will not study	you won't study
he will not come	he won't come
she will not go	she won't go
we will not write	we won't write
they will not read	they won't read

Examples:

It**'ll be** sunny tomorrow.

It **won't** rain.

Will it **be** cooler than today?

It**'s going to** be sunny tomorrow.

It **isn't going to** rain.

Is it **going to be** cooler than today?

Practice A   With a partner, read about the environment. Then make predictions for the future.

The Environment

The environment is a great worry to a growing number of people in countries all over the world. There are many serious problems. These problems didn't exist one hundred years ago. If we don't do something about these environmental problems soon, our planet will not survive as we know it.

These are just some of the environmental problems. There is a great deal of air pollution in the big cities. Damage is appearing in the ozone above the earth. There is a lot of acid rain in the industrialized countries. This is killing lakes and forests all over the world.

People are cutting down forests. They are using farmland to build houses. They are destroying some plant and animal species forever. Many animals, such as the tiger and the elephant, are in danger of disappearing, too.

The large cities in the industrialized countries are running out of room for garbage disposal. Dangerous chemicals and waste are polluting drinking water in many countries. Accidental oil spills are killing fish and birds in many regions.

What do you think will happen in the next ten years? Write about:

Air pollution _____

_____

Farmland _____

_____

Forests _____

_____

Garbage _____

_____

Animals _____

_____

What are two environmental problems that you worry about? What will you do about these problems? Get the same information from your partner.

ME

PROBLEMS	SOLUTIONS
1. _____	_____
2. _____	_____

MY PARTNER

PROBLEMS	SOLUTIONS
1. _____	_____
2. _____	_____

Practice B   At the beginning of the new year, many radio and television stations invite famous seers to make predictions for the future year.
Imagine you are a seer. Make predictions about some of these topics. Then find out your partner's predictions.

TOPICS

you	your teacher	your school
your city	your country	a famous entertainer
a famous politician	the economy	women's fashions
men's fashions	medicine	sports

MY PREDICTIONS

_____

_____

_____

_____

MY PARTNER'S PREDICTIONS

_____

_____

_____

_____

Report your partner's predictions. As you listen to your classmates, decide which predictions will come true.

Practice C   Work with a group. Choose six topics and make predictions about what your group thinks will happen by the year 2010.

TOPICS	SOME VERBS TO USE	SOME ADJECTIVES TO USE
jobs	increase	popular
cigarettes	decrease	better
cars	improve	worse
inflation	get	obsolete
computers	ban	indispensable
taxes	tax	complex
immigration	control	tolerant
plane travel		
politics		
religion		
population growth		
music		
the English language		
men		
women		
science and technology		

My Group's Predictions:

1. _____

2. _____

3. _____

4. _____

5. _____

6. _____

Listen to the other groups' predictions. Write down one prediction you agree with and one you don't agree with.

I agree that _____

I don't agree that _____

Practice D   Work with a group. Predict which things will cost more and which things will cost less by the year 2010. Give reasons for your decisions.

ITEMS

food	computers	oil	water
cigarettes	paper products	houses	hospital care
car telephones	alcoholic beverages	fish	fur coats
education	automobiles	VCR's	public transportation
electrical power	meat	gold	compact disks

MORE EXPENSIVE	REASON	LESS EXPENSIVE	REASON
_____	_____	_____	_____
_____	_____	_____	_____
_____	_____	_____	_____
_____	_____	_____	_____
_____	_____	_____	_____
_____	_____	_____	_____
_____	_____	_____	_____

Write about two things that will cost more and two things that will cost less in the future.

1. _____

2. _____

3. _____

4. _____

FUTURE TIME: *WILL*

Explanation   In addition to predicting, we use *will* . . . to express a promise.

Examples: We'll be home early.
I'll get there as soon as possible.
You won't be sorry you bought this car.
Will you marry me?

Practice A   Work with a partner. Use *will* . . . in these sentences.

1. Andrew promises to be on time. _____ *Andrew will be on time.* _____

2. He promises to do his homework from now on. _____

3. He promises not to cheat. _____

4. The students promise not to make a lot of noise. _____

5. We promise not to stay out late. _____

6. I promise to pick you up after school. _____

7. David promises not to drink too much. _____

8. Nicole promises to save more money. _____

9. We all promise to study harder. _____

10. I promise to turn the music down. _____

11. Do you promise to give up smoking? _____

12. Do you promise to tell the truth from now on? _____

13. He promises to do the dishes if she cooks. _____

14. I promise to meet you later. _____

15. She promises not to get into trouble. _____

16. Does Michael promise to pay back the loan? _____

Make two promises to your classmates:

1. _____

2. _____

Lesson 15   FUTURE TIME: *WILL*

Explanation   We use *will* . . . when we expect something will happen.

      Examples: We expect it to be warm tomorrow.
                     It**'ll be** warm tomorrow.
                     I expect the teacher to know the answer.
                     The teacher **will know** the answer.

Practice A   Work with a partner. Use *will* . . . in these sentences.

1. We expect the weather to be hot in July. ___*The weather'll be hot in July.*___

2. Do you expect the test to be easy? _____

3. We expect the plane to land at 7 P.M.. _____

4. We don't expect it to snow in June. _____

5. They expect the pollution to get worse. _____

6. Do they expect to spend a lot of money? _____

7. I don't expect him to come back to the U.S.A. _____

8. Do you expect them to get married soon? _____

9. We expect him to be back by 2:15. _____

10. We expect her to find a good job. _____

11. I expect the doctor to see her soon. _____

12. Do you expect the English books to be expensive? _____

13. We don't expect the work to be difficult. _____

14. I expect the movie to be exciting. _____

15. We expect them to be polite and friendly. _____

16. I don't expect the concert to be long. _____

17. We expect her to get better quickly. _____

18. We don't expect her to do the shopping. _____

19. I expect everyone to help out. _____

What do you expect about the following things?

The next test: _____

The next holiday: _____

FUTURE TIME: *WILL*

Explanation   We use *will* . . . when we are making an offer.

        Examples: **I'll drive** you to the store.
                       We'**ll cut** the grass for you.
                       I'll get the bill.

Practice A   Work with a partner. Make offers using *will* . . . .

1. Let me get the door for you. _____ *I'll get the door for you.* _____

2. Let us carry the groceries for you. _____

3. Let me cook supper. _____

4. Let us clean up the kitchen for you. _____

5. Let us take out the garbage for you. _____

6. Let me open the window for you. _____

7. Let me turn down the heat for you. _____

8. Let us put away the dishes for you. _____

9. Let us sweep the floor for you. _____

10. Let us set the table. _____

11. Let me get the phone. _____

12. Let me spell my name for you. _____

13. Let me help you with your English. _____

14. Let me explain this word. _____

15. Let me fill out the application form for you. _____

Here are some other expressions for making an offer:

Would you like me to . . .?   Would you like me to make coffee?
Do you want me to . . .?   Do you want me to make coffee?

Make an offer to your partner.

_____

Explanation   We use *will* . . . or the **simple present tense** with a **future time expression** to indicate future time when we are talking about scheduled events.

> **Examples:**   The train **leaves** at 5 o'clock **tonight.**
> The train **will leave** at 5 o'clock tonight.
> The new secretary **starts next week.**
> The new secretary **will start** next week.
> We **have** a test **at the end of the month.**
> We **will have** a test at the end of the month.

Practice A. The Montreal-Toronto Train

Work with a partner. Use the **simple present tense** in the story.

The Montreal-Toronto train run (be) _____ the busiest in Canada. The trip (take)

_____ about five hours. The train (be) _____ always heavily booked. The train

(travel) _____ through the most populated part of the country.

Tomorrow morning, the train (leave) _____ Montreal, in the province of Quebec,

at 10:30. This train (travel) _____ to Toronto in the province of Ontario. It (make)

_____ a number of stops on its way to Toronto.

After it (leave) _____ Montreal tomorrow, the train (pick up) _____ more

passengers at Dorval, in Quebec, and then it (continue) _____ along its route. It (stop)

_____ again at Cornwall, in Ontario. It (take) _____ on more passengers here.

The train attendants (serve) _____ lunch just after the Cornwall stop at approximate-

ly 12 o'clock.

The next stop (be) _____ Brockville, a prosperous little town in eastern Ontario.

Two and a half hours later, the train (get) _____ into Kingston. Kingston is a city of

almost half a million people. Many passengers (get) _____ on here, and a great many

others (get) _____ off at Kingston. After that, there (be) _____ several more stops

before Toronto. The Montreal train (pull) _____ into Toronto's Union Station at 3:30

tomorrow afternoon.

Write TRUE or FALSE.

The train will leave Montreal at half past ten.   **true**

The train will be almost full.   _____

All the passengers on the train will get lunch.   _____

The train will stop in Cornwall after lunch.   _____

Kingston is a city in Quebec.   _____

Toronto is a city in Ontario.   _____

Montreal is a city in Ontario.   _____

The name of the train station in Toronto is Union Station.   _____

Most of the people in Canada live in Ontario and Quebec.   _____

There will be a lot of empty seats on the Toronto-Montreal train. _____

Practice B   Work with a partner. Write down three things you have on your schedule in the near future. Talk about appointments, exams, visits, trips, parties, and other events.

ME	MY PARTNER
_____	_____
_____	_____
_____	_____
_____	_____
_____	_____
_____	_____

Lesson 18   USING *CAN* TO EXPRESS ABILITY

Explanation   We use *can* to express ability.

Examples:

AFFIRMATIVE	INTERROGATIVE	NEGATIVE
He can work.	Can he work? When can he work?	He cannot work. He can't work.
We can sing.	Can we sing? What can we sing?	We cannot sing. We can't sing.
They can play.	Can they play? What can they play?	They cannot play. They can't play.
You can run.	Can you run? How fast can you run?	You cannot run. You can't run.

Pronunciation Note   *Can* is not stressed. We don't pronounce it as loudly or as long as the following verb.

> She can **dance.**
> They can **help** you.
> You can **do** it if you try.

Can't is stressed. We pronounce it louder and longer than *can.*

> I can **float** but I **can't swim.**
> He can **sing** but he **can't whistle.**

Don't stress *can.* Otherwise people will think you are saying *can't.*

Practice A   By yourself, make statements about your abilities. Use these verbs.

1. dance   *I can dance but I can't dance the tango.*

2. cook   *I can cook but I can't cook Chinese food.*

3. sing   _____ *but* _____

4. write   _____ *but* _____

5. speak   _____ *but* _____

6. buy   _____ *but* _____

7. understand   _____ *but* _____

8. play   _____ *but* _____

9. make   _____ *but* _____

10. swim   _____ *but* _____

11. use   _____ *but* _____

12. _____   _____ *but* _____

13. _____   _____ *but* _____

Find out three things your partner can do.

1. _____

2. _____

3. _____

Find out three things your partner can't do.

1. _____

2. _____

3. _____

Practice B   Talk to as many classmates as possible. Ask these questions:

> How many languages can you speak?
> What sport or game can you play?
> What special ability do you have?

	NAME	LANGUAGES	SPORT OR GAME	SPECIAL ABILITY
1.				
2.				
3.				
4.				
5.				
6.				
7.				
8.				
9.				
10.				
11.				
12.				
13.				

Write down the two most interesting answers.

1. _____

2. _____

Practice C   With a partner, match the tool or appliance with what you can do with it.

a saw	dries hair
a hammer	cuts wood
a wrench	cleans carpets
a screwdriver	holds a car up
a paint brush	holds paper together
a jack	spreads paint
a vacuum cleaner	drives nails into wood
plastic wrap	turns screws
a can opener	keeps food fresh
a hairdryer	mixes food
a blender	dries clothing
a dryer	washes dishes
a dishwasher	opens cans
scotch tape	loosens large bolts

Choose eight tools or appliances. Write statements about them. Use *can*.

1. _____ *You can cut wood with a saw.* _____

2. _____

3. _____

4. _____

5. _____

6. _____

7. _____

8. _____

Work with a partner. List five tools or appliances that you **can't do without** and what they do. Then get the same information from your partner.

Example: I can't do without my blender, because I can prepare food with it.

ME

1. _____

2. _____

3. _____

4. _____

5. _____

MY PARTNER

1. _____

2. _____

3. _____

4. _____

5. _____

Practice D   Work with a partner. Match the abilities to the occupation. Then make statements with *can*, and add another ability.

take blood pressure	mechanic
change the oil in a car	nursing assistant
enter data on a computer	chef
operate X-ray equipment	bartender
analyze blood samples	veterinarian
repair VCR's	tailor
do accounting	graphic artist
fill prescriptions	data entry clerk
design signs	accountant
make suits	electronics technician
look after sick animals	laboratory technician
make cocktails	X-ray technologist
plan menus	pharmacist

1. _____ *A nursing assistant can take blood pressure and she can give injections.* _____

2. _____

3. _____

4. _____

5. _____

6. _____

7. _____

8. _____

Practice E   Answer these questions:

What was your last job? _____

What ability do you have? _____

Talk to as many classmates as possible. Find out the same information.

	NAME	LAST JOB	ABILITY
1.			
2.			
3.			
4.			
5.			
6.			

	NAME	LAST JOB	ABILITY
7.	_____		
8.	_____		
9.	_____		
10.	_____		
11.	_____		
12.	_____		
13.	_____		
14.	_____		
15.	_____		

Practice F   Talk to the other people in your class. Find someone who fits these descriptions. Then write that person's name.

Find someone who:

                                                                NAME

can whistle. _____

can play an instrument. _____

can drive a car. _____

can use a computer. _____

can speak three languages. _____

can dance the tango. _____

can change a flat tire. _____

can play tennis. _____

can say their first name backwards. _____

can bake a cake. _____

can't swim. _____

can say, "I love you" in four languages. _____

can't do 20 push-ups. _____

can run two kilometers. _____

can't sew. _____

can draw. _____

Practice G   Work with a partner. Use *can* or *can't* in these sentences.

1. _Can_ you speak German?

2. My friend _____ cook Italian food very well, but his wife _____ .

3. Mice _____ fly, but birds _____ .

4. _____ you teach me to speak Chinese?

5. A camel _____ go without water for a long time.

6. Jessica _____ read small print without glasses.

7. She _____ knit but her husband _____ .

8. Cats are color-blind. They _____ see colors.

9. I have no sense of rhythm. I _____ dance very well.

10. He _____ walk quickly because his leg is in a cast.

11. You _____ figure out this difficult problem without a calculator.

12. They _____ change a tire without a jack.

13. You need a receipt or else you _____ return this merchandise.

14. The secretary _____ use the word processor but the manager _____ .

15. I _____ lend you any money because I'm short of cash.

16. Please print. I _____ read your writing.

17. The clerk _____ use a typewriter but she _____ use a computer.

18. How many languages _____ Christopher speak?

19. What _____ I do for you? I'm afraid you _____ help me today.

20. He's very fit. He _____ do 100 push-ups.

21. The teacher _____ speak both English and French.

22. You _____ see the patient because visiting hours are over.

23. Visitors _____ work in the U.S.A. without a special permit.

24. The dentist _____ see you right away, but he _____ see you next week.

Lesson 19 USING *COULD* TO EXPRESS ABILITY IN THE PAST

Explanation   The past form of *can* is *could*.

Examples: David **can** swim well now.
David **could** swim well **many years ago.**

Can you cook Chinese food?
Could you cook Chinese food **before?**

Sharon **can't** sing very well.
Sharon **couldn't** sing very well **as a child.**

AFFIRMATIVE	INTERROGATIVE	NEGATIVE
I could swim	Could I swim Where could I swim?	I could not swim. I couldn't swim.
He could draw.	Could he draw? What could he draw?	He could not draw. He couldn't draw.
They could dance.	Could they dance? Where could they dance?	They could not dance. They couldn't dance.
Michael could work.	Could Michael work? Where could Michael work?	Michael could not work. Michael couldn't work.

Practice A   What are two things you **could** do before you moved here, that you **can't** do now?

1. _____

2. _____

What are two things you **couldn't** do in your hometown that you **can** do now?

1. _____

2. _____

Get this information from the other people in your class.

NAME	WHAT COULD YOU DO BEFORE?	WHAT COULDN'T YOU DO BEFORE?
1.		
2.		
3.		
4.		
5.		
6.		
7.		

NAME	WHAT COULD YOU DO BEFORE?	WHAT COULDN'T YOU DO BEFORE?
8. _____		
9. _____		
10. _____		
11. _____		
12. _____		
13. _____		
14. _____		
15. _____		

What is the most important thing people could do before?

_____

Lesson 20 | *TO BE ABLE TO*

Explanation   *To be able to . . .* has the same meaning as *can:* ability.

PRESENT TENSE:

AFFIRMATIVE	INTERROGATIVE	NEGATIVE
I am able to go.	Am I able to go?	I am not able to go.
He is able to go.	Is he able to go?	He is not able to go.
She is able to go.	Is she able to go?	She is not able to go.
We are able to go.	Are we able to go?	We are not able to go.
You are able to go.	Are you able to go?	You are not able to go.
They are able to go.	Are they able to go?	They are not able to go.

CONTRACTIONS		CONTRACTIONS
I'm able to go.		I'm not able to go.
He's able to go.		He isn't able to go.
She's able to go.		She isn't able to go.
We're able to go.		We aren't able to go.
You're able to go.		You aren't able to go.
They're able to go.		They aren't able to go.

PAST TENSE:

AFFIRMATIVE	INTERROGATIVE	NEGATIVE
I was able to go.	Was I able to go?	I wasn't able to go.
He was able to go.	Was he able to go?	He wasn't able to go.
She was able to go.	Was she able to go?	She wasn't able to go.
We were able to go.	Were we able to go?	We weren't able to go.
You were able to go.	Were you able to go?	You weren't able to go.
They were able to go.	Were they able to go?	They weren't able to go.

Practice A   Work with a partner. Use *to be able to* . . . in these sentences.

1. Adam couldn't pass the test. _____ *Adam wasn't able to pass the test.* _____

2. Sarah could sing very well. _____

3. The police can control the demonstration. _____

4. Marie can't type very quickly. _____

5. The students can do this exercise. _____

6. She couldn't understand the computer program. _____

7. Can you dance to this music? _____

8. Can cats survive in the wilderness? _____

9. He can't explain the meaning of the word. _____

10. Scientists can't find a cure for cancer. _____

11. I can't follow you when you speak quickly. _____

12. I couldn't hear that word. _____

13. Could Helen play the piano as a child? _____

14. Can elephants run very quickly? _____

15. Human beings can't communicate with animals. _____

16. People with allergies can't eat certain foods. _____

17. She couldn't drink the water in that country. _____

18. Could you dance the twist when you were a teenager? _____

19. Don't walk so fast. I can't keep up with you. _____

20. The doctor couldn't help her. _____

21. We can offer you a good position. _____

22. They couldn't pay him a high salary. _____

Explanation   These are some ways to ask for permission and some responses:

ASKING FOR PERMISSION	POSITIVE RESPONSE	NEGATIVE RESPONSE
May I . . .?	Certainly!	No, I'm sorry.
Can I . . .?	Of course.	I'm afraid not.
May we . . .?	Sure!	No, you can't.
Can we . . .?	No problem.	No way!

Practice A   Work with a partner. Make requests for permission and responses in these situations. Then role play two situations.

1. You want to park in the teachers' parking lot today.

Request: *May I park in the teachers' parking lot today?*

Response: *No, I'm afraid not. This lot is only for the staff.*

2. You want to use the staff restroom.

Request: _____

Response: _____

3. You want to leave class a little early today.

Request: _____

Response: _____

4. You want to call your partner up after 11 P.M. tonight.

Request: _____

Response: _____

5. You want to borrow your partner's notes.

Request: _____

Response: _____

6. You want to change your English class.

Request: _____

Response: _____

7. You want to use the teachers' photocopier.

Request: _____

Response: _____

8. You want to tape-record your English class.

Request: _____

Response: _____

9. You want to bring a friend to sit in on your English class.

Request: _____

Response: _____

10. You want to eat lunch in the classroom.

Request: _____

Response: _____

11. You and your classmates want to have a class party.

Request: _____

Response: _____

12. You want to smoke in the corridor.

Request: _____

Response: _____

13. You and your classmates want to take a class trip.

Request: _____

Response: _____

14. You and your classmates want to take your teacher out for lunch.

Request: _____

Response: _____

15. You want to see the teacher for some extra help after class.

Request: _____

Response: _____

Think of four other requests for permission.

16. Situation: _____

Request: _____

Response: _____

17. Situation: _____

Request: _____

Response: _____

18. Situation: _____

Request: _____

Response: _____

19. Situation: _____

Request: _____

Response: _____

Explanation   There are many different ways to make suggestions. These are just a few ways to make suggestions:

It's a good idea to . . .
Why don't you . . .?
You could . . .
You can . . .

Practice A   Work with a partner. Pick out five situations from the list below and then make suggestions about them. Use two different forms to make suggestions. Role play two situations.

Example:

Your friend's hair is very, very long.

Why don't you try a shorter hairstyle?

You could try a shorter hairstyle.

Situations:

1. Your friend's out of cash and doesn't have time to go the bank.
2. Your friend's got a terrible headache.
3. Your friend has very high phone bills. He makes a lot of long distance calls.
4. Your friend is overweight and out of shape.
5. Your friend lives in a dangerous neighborhood.
6. Your friend can't read the teacher's writing on the blackboard.
7. Your friend can't get into university because his English is poor.
8. It takes your friend three hours to get to school by bus.
9. Your friend's neighbors play loud music at all hours.

Suggestions:

_____

_____

_____

_____

_____

_____

_____

_____

_____

_____

Practice B   What's your biggest problem in learning English? Ask your partner for suggestions.

Problem: _____

Suggestion: _____

Think of two other problems you have. Ask your partner for suggestions. Then find out your partner's problems and make suggestions.

My partner's problems:

1. _____

2. _____

My suggestions:

1. _____

2. _____

Explanation   Some verbs in English can take both a **direct** and an **indirect object.**

Examples:

	DIRECT OBJECT	INDIRECT OBJECT
He gave	the book	to the student.
She taught	English	to the engineering class.

Most of the time, we can state the **indirect object** in two ways:

He gave the book **to the student.**

> **or**

He gave **the student** the book.

She taught English **to the engineering class.**

> **or**

She taught **the engineering class** English.

But be careful with **pronouns.**

He gave **it** to the student.	**Can NOT be:**	He gave the student it.
She taught **it** to them.	**Can NOT be:**	She taught them it.

Here are some verbs that take **indirect objects:**

give something **to** someone	or	give someone something
write something **to** someone	or	write someone something
send something **to** someone	or	send someone something
lend something **to** someone	or	lend someone something
take something **to** someone	or	take someone something
show something **to** someone	or	show someone something
teach something **to** someone	or	teach someone something
buy something **for** someone	or	buy someone something
make something **for** someone	or	make someone something
leave something **for** someone	or	leave someone something
bring something **for** someone	or	bring someone something
bake something **for** someone	or	bake someone something

Practice A. Christmas in the U.S.A.

Work with a partner. Read this story and underline the indirect objects. Then write the story again. Use indirect objects without prepositions.

Christmas is a special holiday in many countries. In North America, it is the biggest holiday celebration of the year. In the U.S.A., most people spend the month of December getting ready for Christmas. These people send Christmas cards to their friends and relatives. They write letters to their loved ones abroad, and they usually send special Christmas parcels to them.

Christmas is a time for thinking about others. Most people buy gifts for their family and friends. A lot of people like to make special presents for their friends and relatives. Some people knit sweaters and scarves for their relatives. Others bake Christmas cakes for their neighbors or make personalized gifts for them. On the night before Christmas, everyone wraps their presents and places them under the Christmas tree. In the middle of the night, Santa Claus arrives. He brings presents for everyone. The children leave cookies and milk for him. They don't want Santa Claus to get hungry or tired out.

On Christmas Day, everyone, especially the children, gets up very early. They open their gifts with excitement. They show their presents to each other, and the happy holiday spirit fills the air. Later in the day, the chef of the family will make a special Christmas dinner for everyone.

_____

_____

_____

_____

_____

_____

_____

_____

_____

Describe a special holiday in your country.

What is the holiday? _____

Who do people give gifts to? _____

Who do people make things for? _____

Who do people send cards to? _____

What other things do people do? _____

_____

_____

Find out the same information from your partner.

_____

_____

_____

_____

Practice B   Work with a partner. Write these sentences with indirect objects a different way, if possible.

1. Michael gave the present to Sarah. _____ *Michael gave Sarah the present.* _____

2. The policeman gave the driver a ticket. _____

3. We'll send it to her. _____

4. James sent his girlfriend flowers. _____

5. The students took a gift to the teacher. _____

6. I brought a cup of coffee for you. _____

7. His wife makes supper for him. _____

8. She baked him a birthday cake. _____

9. He bought them for his father. _____

10. They lent it to their friends. _____

11. We wrote letters to our classmates. _____

12. She taught the class an important lesson. _____

13. They left me a lot of work. _____

14. Show your driver's license to me. _____

15. They gave it to David. _____

16. Why don't you sell it to me? _____

17. She'll show it to you. _____

Explanation   Here are some question forms and short answers:

QUESTIONS	SHORT ANSWERS	
Do you live near the school?	Yes, I do.	or No, I don't.
Have you got a car?	Yes, I have.	or No, I haven't.
Are you chewing gum?	Yes, I am.	or No, I'm not.
Did you go to bed late last night?	Yes, I did.	or No, I didn't.
Will you help us?	Yes, I will.	or No, I won't.
Are you going to go out tonight?	Yes, I am.	or No, I'm not.
Can you speak French?	Yes, I can.	or No, I can't.
Could you speak English before?	Yes, I could.	or No, I couldn't.
Are you able to drive?	Yes, I am.	or No, I'm not.
Were you able to swim as a child?	Yes, I was.	or No, I wasn't.

Practice A   Ask the people in your class these questions. When you find someone who fits the description, write that person's name down. Remember to use the correct question form.

Find someone in the class who:

NAME

can eat a whole pizza. _____

is going to take a trip soon. _____

couldn't speak English one year ago. _____

didn't have breakfast today. _____

went out last night. _____

won't tell you their age. _____

has an apartment. _____

is moving soon. _____

will take public transportation home. _____

can speak three languages. _____

doesn't drive. _____

was at a shopping mall recently. _____

bought something recently. _____

is going to study tonight. _____

has got a cold. _____

can't swim. _____

has got a pet. _____

was able to pass the driver's test. _____

is able to understand baseball. _____

has got a part-time job. _____

is wearing black socks. _____

won't sleep in on Saturday morning. _____

enjoys English classes. _____

Lesson 25   PAST CONTINUOUS TENSE

Explanation

The **past continuous tense** expresses an action that was continuing at a specific point in the past.

Example:

Last night Diane did her homework until 8 P.M. Then she took a bath.

7 P.M.   8 P.M.   8:30 P.M.

        homework   bath

At 7:30 Diane **was doing** her homework. **At 8:15** she **was taking** a bath.

We form the **past continuous tense** by using the **past tense** of the verb *to be* and by adding *ing* to the verb stem. These are the forms of the **past continuous tense:**

AFFIRMATIVE	INTERROGATIVE	WITH QUESTION WORDS
I was sleeping	Was I sleeping?	Why was I sleeping?
he was sleeping	Was he sleeping?	Where was he sleeping?
she was sleeping	Was she sleeping?	Why was she sleeping?
it was sleeping	Was it sleeping?	Where was it sleeping?
we were sleeping	Were we sleeping?	Why were we sleeping?
you were sleeping	Were you sleeping?	Why were you sleeping?
they were sleeping	Were they sleeping?	Why were they sleeping?

NEGATIVES	CONTRACTIONS
I was not sleeping	I wasn't sleeping
he was not sleeping	he wasn't sleeping
she was not sleeping	she wasn't sleeping
it was not sleeping	it wasn't sleeping
we were not sleeping	we weren't sleeping
you were not sleeping	you weren't sleeping
they were not sleeping	they weren't sleeping

Practice A. The Basic English Class

Work with a partner. Read the story. What were the students doing at the times listed?

Yesterday was a very busy day for the Basic English class. At 9:30 in the morning, they had their weekly grammar test. After the test, they took a fifteen-minute coffee break. Then from 10:45 until 11:45 they worked in the computer lab. They wrote stories. At 11:45 they all went out together to a Chinese restaurant for lunch. They got back at 12:45. Then they did a listening comprehension test until 1:30 P.M. From 1:45 until 3:00 P.M. they practiced speaking English in the conversation class. After that they worked on special projects in the library until 3:30. When they left the school just before 4 P.M. they were all glad the day was over.

At 9:30 A.M. _____ *they were having a grammar test.* _____

At 10:40 A.M. _____

At 11:00 A.M. _____

At 12:00 P.M. _____

At 1:00 P.M. _____

At 2:00 P.M. _____

At 3:15 P.M. _____

Practice B

Work with a partner. Choose a day in the recent past. List all the things your English class did.

_____   _____

_____   _____

_____   _____

Pick three specific times on that day. What was your class doing?

TIME   ACTIVITY

_____

_____

_____

Practice C. Diane's Datebook

Work with a partner. Read the page from Diane's datebook. Then write what she was doing at the times listed.

TUESDAY, FEBRUARY 3

Morning	9:00–10:00	Take car to garage for check-up
	10:00–11:00	Teach basic computer class
	11:00–12:00	Make up exam for computer class
	12:00–1:00	Lunch with principal
Afternoon	1:00–2:00	Pick up car at garage
	2:00–3:00	Teach intermediate computer class
	3:00–4:00	Give basic computer class a test
	4:00–5:00	Mark tests
Evening	7:00–9:00	Meet Ellen for supper at the Blue Moon Cafe

1. At 9:30 _____ *she was taking her car to the garage.* _____

2. At 10:15 _____

3. At 11:45 _____

4. At 12:30 _____

5. At 1:45 _____

6. At 2:15 _____

7. At 3:50 _____

8. At 4:30 _____

9. At 7:30 _____

By yourself, list what you did on a specific date.

DATE: _____
TIME   ACTIVITY

_____

_____

_____

_____

Work with a partner. Exchange information about what you were doing.

	ME	MY PARTNER
In the morning:	_____	_____
In the afternoon:	_____	_____
In the evening:	_____	_____

Practice D   Talk to as many people in your class as possible. Ask these questions:

> What were you doing at 8 P.M. last night?
> What were you doing at 9:30 in the evening last Saturday night?

	NAME	8:00 P.M. LAST NIGHT	9:30 LAST SATURDAY NIGHT
1.			
2.			
3.			
4.			
5.			
6.			
7.			
8.			
9.			
10.			
11.			
12.			

NAME	8:00 P.M. LAST NIGHT	9:30 LAST SATURDAY NIGHT
13. _____		
14. _____		
15. _____		

What was the most interesting activity last Saturday night?

_____

Practice E   Talk to as many people in the class as possible. Ask these questions:

> Where were you living three years ago?
> What were you doing?
> What was happening there at that time? (one important thing)

	NAME	PLACE	ACTIVITY	EVENT
1.	_____			
2.	_____			
3.	_____			
4.	_____			
5.	_____			
6.	_____			
7.	_____			
8.	_____			
9.	_____			
10.	_____			
11.	_____			
12.	_____			
13.	_____			
14.	_____			
15.	_____			

Explanation   Adverbs give information about the action of the verb. A large group of adverbs have the ending *ly*. These are adverbs of manner.

Examples:

slow<u>ly</u>	angri<u>ly</u>
quick<u>ly</u>	quiet<u>ly</u>

We form these adverbs by adding *ly* to the adjective.

Examples:

ADJECTIVE	ADVERB
beautiful	beautifully
slow	slowly
quick	quickly
angry	angrily
quiet	quietly

The main exceptions are:

ADJECTIVE	ADVERB
hard	hard
fast	fast
good	well

Spelling Note   When the adjective ends in a consonant and *y*, we change the *y* to *i* and then we add the *ly* ending.

Examples:

happ<u>y</u>	happ<u>i</u>ly
nois<u>y</u>	nois<u>i</u>ly

Practice A. Diane's Sister

With your partner, rewrite these statements. Use adverbs.

Diane's sister, Ellen, is an extraordinary person.
She does almost everything very well.

1. Ellen is a beautiful singer. _____ *She sings beautifully.* _____

2. Ellen is a graceful dancer. _____

3. Ellen is a good cook. _____

4. Ellen is a careful driver. _____

5. Ellen is a hard worker. _____

6. Ellen is a quick thinker. _____

7. Ellen is a good listener. _____

8. Ellen is a stylish dresser. _____

9. Ellen is a tactful speaker. _____

10. Ellen is a fast reader. _____

11. Ellen is a neat writer. _____

12. Ellen is an intelligent writer. _____

13. Ellen is a good tennis player. _____

14. Ellen is a wise money manager. _____

Write three things about one of your relatives. Use adverbs. Then get the same information from your partner.

MY _____   MY PARTNER'S _____

_____   _____

_____   _____

_____   _____

Practice B   Work with a partner. Describe actions of the people in your class. Use the adverbs listed.

1. hard   *The teacher works hard.* _____

2. well   _____

3. carefully   _____

4. quickly   _____

5. quietly   _____

6. clearly   _____

7. neatly   _____

8. easily   _____

9. fast   _____

10. slowly   _____

Practice C   Write down three things you do well. Then write down three things you do badly. Exchange this information with your partner.

Me:

WELL   BADLY

1. _____   _____

2. _____   _____

3. _____   _____

My partner:

WELL   BADLY

1. _____   _____

2. _____   _____

3. _____   _____

Lesson 27 | # COMPARATIVES AND SUPERLATIVES: MAKING COMPARISONS

Explanation   Adjectives of two or more syllables use a special structure for the comparative and the superlative forms.

Comparative:

An elephant is **more** intelligent **than** an ant.
An ant is **less** intelligent **than** an elephant.
An ant isn't **as** intelligent **as** an elephant.

Superlative:

Human beings are **the most** intelligent creatures of all.
Lobsters are **the least** intelligent creatures I can think of.

Practice A   Work with a partner. For each sentence, make two comparative statements.

1. Carnations aren't as expensive as roses.

Roses are more expensive than carnations.
_____
Carnations are less expensive than roses.
_____

2. Carnations aren't as beautiful as roses.

_____

_____

3. Dogs aren't as curious as cats.

_____

_____

4. Dogs aren't as independent as cats.

_____

_____

5. Cats aren't as good-natured as dogs.

_____

_____

6. Cats aren't as friendly as dogs.

_____

_____

7. Cats aren't as loyal as dogs.

_____

_____

8. Sharks aren't as intelligent as dolphins.

_____

_____

9. Whales aren't as dangerous as sharks.

_____

_____

10. Ducks aren't as graceful as swans.

_____

_____

11. Typewriters aren't as useful as computers.

_____

_____

12. Telephones aren't as expensive as fax machines.

_____

_____

13. Newspapers aren't as interesting as magazines.

_____

_____

14. Books aren't as exciting as movies.

_____

_____

15. Men aren't as careful as women.

_____

_____

16. Children aren't as cautious as adults.

_____

_____

17. Money isn't as important as health.

_____

_____

Practice B With a partner, make a comparative and a superlative statement. Use the adjectives and the nouns.

1. expensive   streetcar ride   bicycle ride   taxi ride

   A streetcar ride is more expensive than a bicycle ride.

   A taxi ride is the most expensive of all.

2. expensive   train trip   bus trip   plane trip

   _____

   _____

3. dangerous   car travel   plane travel   train travel

   _____

   _____

4. enjoyable   plane trip   boat trip   bus trip

_____

_____

5. comfortable   bus ride   motorcycle ride   taxi ride

_____

_____

6. crowded   trains   planes   subways

_____

_____

7. convenient   taxis   buses   subways

_____

_____

8. relaxing   bus trip   car trip   subway trip

_____

_____

9. stressful   plane travel   bus travel   car travel

_____

_____

10. interesting   train trip   boat trip   plane trip

_____

_____

Practice C   By yourself, compare public transportation in your country with public transportation in North America. Then exchange this information with your partner.

My comparisons:

_____

_____

_____

My partner's comparisons:

_____

_____

_____

Practice D Compare life in your country with life in North America. Talk about the prices, jobs, sports and entertainment, housing, family life.

My comparisons:

_____

_____

_____

My partner's comparisons:

_____

_____

_____

Practice E What was the most important event in your life? _____

What was the most enjoyable period in your life? _____

What was the most difficult period in your life? _____

Talk to as many people in the class as possible. Find out the same information from them.

NAME	MOST IMPORTANT EVENT	MOST ENJOYABLE PERIOD	MOST DIFFICULT PERIOD
1.			
2.			
3.			
4.			
5.			
6.			
7.			

NAME	MOST IMPORTANT EVENT	MOST ENJOYABLE PERIOD	MOST DIFFICULT PERIOD
8.			
9.			
10.			
11.			
12.			
13.			
14.			
15.			

What are two of the most interesting answers?

_____

_____

Practice F. Deltiology

Read this with a partner, and answer the questions.

Collecting Postcards

Are you like me? Do you have drawers full of old postcards? Do you hate to throw out scenes of sunny beaches and romantic little villages in exotic faraway countries?

If you are like me, you love to receive postcards from anywhere in the world. But did you know that collecting postcards is an important hobby? It is called *deltiology* and it is the third largest collecting hobby in the world. The most popular collecting hobby is stamp collecting. The second most popular is collecting coins.

The first postcards came out in Austria in 1869. Britain issued postcards in 1872. People began to collect cards almost from the beginning. Today, postcards are available all over the globe. However, many people are still collecting them. They are also selling them. In fact, some postcards can bring very high prices. The most expensive selling price for a postcard was $400.00. Susan Brown Nicholson of Lisle, Illinois, sold this card in September 1984. Those of us who hate to clean out our drawers and throw away old postcards can now have a very good excuse not to do so. We can call ourselves deltiologists and claim that we are waiting for postcards to become more valuable.

Work with a partner. Answer these TRUE or FALSE questions.

The oldest postcards come from Austria. _____**true**_____

England produced postcards in 1869. _____

Deltiology is a name for collecting coins. _____

Postcards usually have pictures on them. _____

People send postcards at Christmas and for birthdays. _____

Stamp collecting is as popular as coin collecting. _____

Collecting postcards is the third most popular hobby. _____

Postcard collecting is more popular than stamp collecting. _____

Some postcards can be valuable. _____

The highest price paid for a postcard was $4000.00. _____

The writer is a deltiologist. _____

The writer likes to get postcards. _____

Lesson 28 | COMPARATIVES AND SUPERLATIVES: OPINIONS

Explanation   When we use comparatives or superlatives, we sometimes need to say that these are our opinions. Here are some expressions for stating opinions:

I think . . .	In my opinion . . .
I believe . . .	If you ask me . . .
I feel . . .	I guess . . .

Here are some expressions of agreement and disagreement:

AGREEMENT	DISAGREEMENT
I agree.	I don't agree.
That's what I think, too.	I don't think so.
That's true.	I don't believe that.
Of course!	You can't say that.
Absolutely!	No way!
Certainly!	
I'll say!	

Practice A. Men and Women

Work with a partner. Compare men and women. Use these adjectives. Use opinion statements.

hard-working _____

emotional _____

intelligent _____

practical _____

careless _____

curious _____

talkative _____

independent _____

sensitive _____

powerful _____

reliable _____

fearful _____

funny _____

easy-going _____

helpful _____

strong _____

cautious _____

What is one thing you agreed about?

_____

_____

What is one thing you disagreed about?

_____

_____

Report to the class.

Practice B. Sports

Work with a partner. Make comparative and superlative statements. Use the adjectives. Use opinion statements.

1. dangerous   hockey   baseball   tennis

     We believe baseball is more dangerous than tennis.

     We think hockey is the most dangerous sport of the three.

2. physical   golf   American football   volleyball

3. expensive   golf   tennis   ping-pong

4. exciting   football   soccer   golf

5. violent   boxing   soccer   American football

6. graceful   soccer   hockey   football

7. popular   soccer   hockey   basketball

8. enjoyable   swimming   golf   tennis

9. difficult   skiing   skating   basketball

_____

_____

10. relaxing   tennis   golf   swimming

_____

_____

11. stressful   horse racing   baseball   wrestling

_____

_____

12. interesting   boxing   basketball   baseball

_____

_____

13. tiring   tennis   golf   ping-pong

_____

_____

14. lucrative   baseball   basketball   soccer

_____

_____

15. demanding   horseback riding   swimming   running

_____

_____

16. safe   aerobics   bicycling   baseball

_____

_____

Practice C   Describe the most popular sport in your city. Compare it to some other sports. State your opinion of this sport.

_____

_____

_____

_____

_____

Lesson 29   *THE SAME AS/DIFFERENT FROM*

Explanation   We can show similarities by using the structure *the same as*.

Examples: This word has **the same meaning as** that one.
American spelling is **the same as** British spelling.

We can show differences by using the structure *different from*.

Examples: This word has a **different meaning from** that one.
American English is **different from** British English.

Practice A   Work with a partner. Read this and answer the TRUE or FALSE questions.

American and British Spelling

What are the differences between American English and British English? Everyone knows that these two varieties of English sound different from each other. But if you think about it, you will realize that even people who speak British English sound different from each other depending on where they live. The same thing is true for the Americans. Floridians sound different from New Yorkers, for example.

American words are different from British words. Americans say *truck* and the British say *lorry*. Americans say *elevator* and the British say *lift*. This difference in vocabulary is not as important as some people think, because even in the same region there are often different words for the same thing depending on the speaker's social status, education and age, and the situation.

Think, for example of all the different words for man. *Gentleman, fellow, "guy," "bozo"* are only a few. Think of all the different words for money. *Funds, resources, dough, bucks, "moolah", bread* are only a beginning. We can say that spoken English shows the greatest differences from region to region. Written English shows far fewer differences.

What about British and American spelling? Isn't British spelling different from American spelling? The answer is yes, sometimes, and no—most of the time. The changes in American spelling were the work of Noah Webster. Webster was an important American scholar. He wrote a world-famous dictionary. He wanted to make spelling more simple and to spell words the way they sound.

The spelling system of English, or of any language, is really a tradition and so it is very difficult to change. Most people in the United States were very happy with the standard English spelling of words. They accepted only a handful of Webster's changes. Today, most English dictionaries will give both the American and British spellings of these words. Here are a few examples of the differences:

AMERICAN SPELLING	BRITISH SPELLING
center	centre
color	colour
favorite	favourite
program	programme

Answer TRUE or FALSE.

1. All British people sound the same.

2. New Yorkers sound the same as other Americans.

3. The vocabulary of Americans is completely different from that of British people.

4. The speech of professors is very different from that of teenagers at a party.

5. The biggest differences between American and British English are in speaking.

6. The differences in writing between American and British English are greater than the differences in speaking.

7. "Gentleman" has the same meaning as "guy."

8. "Bread" doesn't have the same meaning as "funds".

9. American spelling isn't very different from British spelling.

10. Webster made changes in spelling because he wanted American English to be different from British English.

11. Webster was able to change American spelling a great deal.

12. One example of Webster's changes is the spelling of "center."

13. It's difficult to change a spelling system.

Practice B   Work with a partner. Talk about those things in your languages that are the same as in English, and those that are different from English.

Me:

Language: _____

SIMILARITIES	DIFFERENCES
_____	_____
_____	_____
_____	_____

My partner: _____

Language: _____

SIMILARITIES   DIFFERENCES

_____   _____

_____   _____

_____   _____

Lesson 30 | REVIEW OF TENSES

Practice A   Work with a partner. Use the correct form of the verb in these sentences.

1. (drive) Marie _____*drove*_____ to work last night.

2. (see) The students _____ a program about water pollution before.

3. (not know) They _____ about this problem a few years ago.

4. (get) Everyone _____ very upset when the show was over.

5. (take) _____ Kevin _____ some medicine a little while ago?

6. (catch) He _____ a bad cold last weekend.

7. (take) We _____ it easy from now on.

8. (leave) The plane _____ at 6 A.M. tomorrow morning.

9. (not forget) Thank you. I _____ your kindness.

10. (speak) Please be quiet. The teacher _____.

11. (start) Please come in. We _____ the test when you arrived.

12. (buy) What a gorgeous jacket! Where _____ you _____ it?

13. (lose) He never listens. One of these days I _____ my temper.

14. (break) Who _____ this expensive crystal ashtray?

15. (do) I promise I _____ this favor for you.

16. (write) They _____ the test at 6:30 last night.

17. (have) _____ Steven _____ an appointment with the dentist tomorrow?

18. (forgive) I'm really sorry. _____ you _____ me?

19. (get) What happened to you? I _____ into an argument with my boss.

20. (sit)   Last month at this time I _____ on the beach in Mexico.

21. (not be able to)   I'm sorry. I _____ get to the bank before it closed.

22. (not ring)   The telephone _____ when I came in.

23. (go)   How _____ it _____ ? Not too bad. I can't complain.

24. (go)   Where _____ they _____ for their next holiday?

25. (hold)   Several men _____ up the bank at closing time yesterday.

26. (watch)   What's on? I _____ the news.

27. (not believe)   That story doesn't scare me. I _____ in ghosts.

28. (not have got)   Please excuse the mess. We _____ time to tidy up.

29. (live)   This is Joshua. He _____ next door to me.

30. (wear)   _____ everybody _____ formal clothes for the dance tonight?

Practice B   With a partner, form questions.

1. The plane takes off at noon. _____ *Does the plane take off at noon?* _____

2. She'll get over the flu in a few days. _____

3. He could speak five languages as a child. _____

4. They were waiting for the teacher. _____

5. Megan threw away all her old files and notes. _____

6. We want her to pay attention to us. _____

7. Andrew's got enough time to finish the test. _____

8. Jessica's working to get enough money for college. _____

9. The nurses 're going to have a meeting. _____

10. He'll get to class on time. _____

11. He found out a lot of information. _____

12. Children are able to operate the computer. _____

13. She's got a toothache. _____

14. They practice their English after school. _____

15. We're leaving right away. _____

16. Justin brought his lunch to school. _____